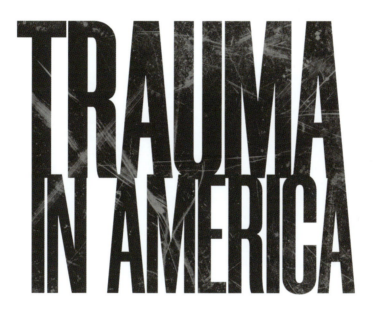

UNDERSTANDING HOW PEOPLE FACE HARDSHIPS AND HOW THE CHURCH OFFERS **HOPE**

Research commissioned by American Bible Society
Philadelphia, Pennsylvania

Research conducted by Barna Group
Ventura, California

Copyright © 2020 by American Bible Society. All rights reserved.

ISBN: 978-1-945269-76-9
ABS item 125023

The information contained in this report is true and accurate to the best knowledge of the copyright holder. It is provided without warranty of any kind: express, implied or otherwise. In no event shall American Bible Society, Barna Group or their officers or employees be liable for any special, incidental, indirect or consequential damages of any kind, or any damages whatsoever resulting from the use of this information, whether or not users have been advised of the possibility of damage, or on any theory of liability, arising out of or in connection with the use of this information.

All Bible quotes from *Good News Translation*® (Today's English Version, Second Edition), copyright © 1992 American Bible Society. All rights reserved.

TABLE OF CONTENTS

5	**PREFACE**
11	**INTRODUCTION**
17	**METHODOLOGY**

CHAPTERS

21	**INCIDENCE OF TRAUMA**
49	**COPING WITH TRAUMA**
63	**WHAT CHURCHES CAN DO**
79	**DEEPENING FAITH DURING TRAUMA**
91	**PASTORS' PREPARATION FOR TRAUMA**

CONCLUSION

107	**WALKING THROUGH TRAUMA WITH THE SCRIPTURES**

APPENDIX

109	**NOTES**
111	**ACKNOWLEDGMENTS**

 Preface

MY EXPERIENCE WITH TRAUMA AND THE BIBLE

BY DAVID KINNAMAN

Barna Group

My team and I have converged in Denver where we are presenting to a client. We've spent the better part of the morning talking through some key research findings.

My phone vibrates. I take a quick look at the screen, mostly to make sure one of my children isn't trying to contact me. It's a text from my wife, Jill.

My headache is killing me. Can you call?

Inwardly, I groan, not because her text represents an interruption, but because this reminder that her pain isn't going away breaks my heart. I hate seeing her like this. Migraines have hounded her for several years, but she's always managed—until, that is, the last month or so, when they've become unbearable.

"Excuse me," I murmur to no one in particular as the presentation continues, and slide into the hallway.

"Jill? Are you OK? What's going on?"

"Dave, these headaches are so bad." She falls silent, struggling to get through the agony, to find her way to the other side of it. Something about her silence tells me it's not just the pain she's trying to navigate; she's not sure how much she wants to worry me.

"Honey, you should just go straight to the ER, OK? They'll give you some pain medication. You need relief from this."

Jill is tough. Always has been. She never draws attention to herself until she's at the end of her rope—which is why, stepping back into the meeting, I find it nearly impossible to concentrate.

Jerry, a friend, asks at the next break what's going on. He can see I'm distracted. I explain what's happening with Jill. He listens and, when I finish, looks me straight in the eye and says, "Dave, you should get on a plane and go home. Your wife needs you."

His words feel like a bucket of cold water, waking me up to reality. I know he's right.

It will be good to be home. It will be good to be with her.

Because I bought this ticket at the last minute, I'm in a middle seat with a large man on either side. I sigh, pull my elbows in, put my headphones on and decide that, as soon as we reach altitude, I'll distract myself with some work.

The ascent out of Denver is rough due to some changing weather, and the bumps pinball me back and forth between my seatmates. When the ride finally smooths out and the seatbelt light turns off, I take out my laptop, feeling preemptive relief at the welcome distraction. I purchase Wi-Fi for the flight; the little icon on my computer lights up. What a miracle of communication it is, that I can be traveling hundreds of miles per hour, tens of thousands of feet off the ground, and have a device in my hand that sends signals into space and back again, keeping me in touch with the people I love.

The connection is successful. A text comes through from Jill, a simple message, a short sentence. It changes my life forever.

"The CAT scan showed that I have a brain tumor."

That was early June 2017, and that calamitous day was the beginning of a season of trauma for Jill and for our family. Since then, Jill has sustained all sorts of medical trauma: brain surgeries, radiation, rounds of chemo, lumbar punctures, infusions, seizures, cancer recurrences and more. But there are other traumas we've all endured: financial, vocational, spiritual, emotional. Our lives have been defined by managing our way through the big and small traumas of caring for her, by the constant effort to find our footing on endlessly changing terrain.

There have been good moments, days and weeks during the last three or so years, too. Trauma makes the good stuff even more precious.

Still, dealing with trauma, living in its long shadow and forging a new normal, has defined our family's experience. I've learned the hard way to better understand the universality of trauma: that to be human is to endure and, by God's grace, to flourish through the macro and micro traumas we call life.

Having grown up in a Christian home—in a pastor's household—I've been a believer in Jesus and a person devoted to his Word for as long as I can remember. At ages six or seven, my sister and I used to record ourselves preaching! I love the Bible at an almost genetic level.

Yet through the ups and downs of Jill's brain cancer, I've had to carve out a new relationship to the Scriptures. At first, for many weeks, I was so shocked and angry and simply overwhelmed, I couldn't even open the Bible. Then, after a period of softening, I opened the Psalms; my hollowness, fears and anger began to find a voice. A few weeks later, I came across a section in 2 Corinthians that spoke deeply to my traumatized heart and soul. I don't remember if someone texted it to me or if I Googled "suffering in the Bible," but I found it and it was a lifeline. At that point, Jill was in ICU and her cognitive function was frighteningly low. All the things I thought I knew were stripped away.

I wrote in my journal that day:

2 Corinthians 1:3–11:

- God is our merciful Father and the source of all comfort.
- He comforts us in all our troubles so we can comfort others.
- For the more we suffer for Christ, the more God will shower us with his comfort through Christ.
- We were crushed and overwhelmed beyond our ability to endure, and we thought we would never live through it ... but as a result, we stopped relying on ourselves and learned to rely only on God, who raises the dead.
- And you are helping us by praying for us.

God doesn't waste our suffering. He walks *with us* through traumatic experiences and trauma-filled seasons—and though I have since experienced his presence and ongoing work for myself, it was making that discovery *first in the Bible* that was a comfort in those painful days.

Just as he has done with so many believers before me, God's Spirit used the Scriptures to minister comfort to my traumatized spirit.

Mine is not a unique experience. The following pages explore what Barna research, commissioned by our partners at American Bible Society, has uncovered among others who have experienced or are experiencing trauma. We pray these findings will bless and inspire you to lean on the Spirit's work through the Bible to heal and comfort those who are hurting.

DAVID KINNAMAN is the author of the bestselling books *Faith For Exiles*, *Good Faith*, *You Lost Me* and *unChristian*. He is president of Barna Group, a leading research and communications company that works with churches, nonprofits and businesses ranging from film studios to financial services. Since 1995, David has directed interviews with more than 1.5 million individuals and overseen hundreds of U.S. and global research studies. He and his wife live in California with their three children.

 Introduction

WHY WE BELIEVE IN THE ROLES OF CHURCH & SCRIPTURE IN TRAUMA HEALING

BY NICOLE MARTIN
American Bible Society

It started with a phone call from a mobile phone, in the forest outside of a little town in northern Congo. Elderly parents calling their adult son in Philadelphia, reporting that a violent militia group had ravaged that town, and they had fled for their safety. That son—Bagudekia Alobeyo—was on the staff of American Bible Society (ABS). He quickly raised funds and arranged for two evacuation flights for his extended family. Once they were resettled safely, Bagudekia's boss, Robert Briggs*, organized a small team to evaluate the conditions within Congo.

That trip in 2010 exposed the team to the harsh reality of trauma. Women, children, men, pastors, truck drivers, teachers … none were spared. Poverty was one thing, but debilitating, destructive violence had crashed through those lives leaving behind wreckage and a future

*Robert Briggs is currently interim president and CEO of American Bible Society.

marked by despair. The team returned home, convinced that the Bible had something to say, but it had to be said differently.

That realization coincided with the discovery of *Healing the Wounds of Trauma: How the Church Can Help,* a book written by staff from SIL International and Wycliffe Bible Translators that had been tested and refined in the field for nearly a decade. That year ABS began working with the authors and other ministry partners to refine and scale the program model and launch the Trauma Healing Institute. The book and the practice of Bible-based trauma healing have swept the world, proving particularly useful among vulnerable and underserved populations. But the Bible offers hope to hurting people everywhere, including in the United States.

Today, in the spring of 2020, the world is caught up in a fight against a pandemic that, at the time of writing, has infected over 3.8 million people and claimed the lives of over 265,000 around the world.[1] The SARS-CoV-2 virus first came to light in late 2019 and coronavirus disease (COVID-19) quickly circled the globe bringing disruption to everything from the global economy to individual families' ability to earn a living, educate their children, celebrate their special days and mourn their dead. Tragically, the virus has proven so contagious that those who succumb to the disease often die alone, separated from their families and loved ones in order to protect public health. The pandemic is still raging. With it comes a need for the church to care for the emotional and spiritual wounds experienced by victims and their families. Wounds not dissimilar from what our brothers and sisters experienced in the Congo 10 years ago.

When we started this research project with Barna Group in the summer of 2019, we had no idea that COVID-19 would be the next traumatic event, but we knew that trauma is a part of the human condition in this fallen world. Since the September 11 attack on the World Trade Center in New York, the U.S. military has seen over 52,800 personnel wounded and nearly 7,000 killed in the Global War on Terrorism. The trauma of repeated deployment has been linked to record rates of suicide among both active duty personnel and veterans. Recent cultural shifts have highlighted the travesty of sexual harassment and violence often experienced by women. Even inside the church, women have been mistreated and too often children have not been safe. Cities in America are still shaken by racial conflict that has its roots in slavery, Jim Crow and redlining (just to name a few). Generations of African Americans have faced oppression, producing a festering wound on America's soul. Misogyny, child abuse, gun violence, extreme poverty and a litany of other ills work together to rob people of hope, often leaving some to define their lives by their trauma. Research into Adverse Childhood Events shows that many lives are actually shortened due to trauma's lasting effects on health and vitality. And this does not include the traumas that individuals face on a regular basis through various disasters, mistreatment, grief and pain.

In this study, we defined trauma narrowly as *physical, psychological or emotional trauma, such as extreme violence, abuse or a near-death experience that produces a response of intense fear, helplessness or horror lasting more than a few weeks*. According to this definition and our findings, one in five American adults has been a victim or witness to events that traumatized them in just the past 10 years.

Thankfully, *awareness* of trauma is growing around the world, including in the U.S. church. Trauma affects every part of a person: mind, body and spirit. It affects individuals and communities, young and old, men and women. Privileged people can experience trauma. So can people who are already the victims of injustice. Trauma, sadly, is part of the human condition.

While some people heal without much intervention, trauma can result in long-term problems not only for individuals but also for their families and communities. Symptoms of trauma can lead to some of the suffering explored in this report: sleeplessness, anxiety, difficulty feeling close to loved ones, intrusive thoughts and more.

As prevalent as it is, trauma can still be hard to talk about, and it can be difficult to know how to help. Many traumatized people also keep their pain hidden. Others would seek help and relief—if they knew where to find it.

ABS desires to look at how hardships and traumatic experiences affect relationships with God, self and others, as well as how the Bible offers hope. This study is meant to give a better picture of trauma among adults in the United States—and where they seek and find healing.

WHY THE CHURCH IS IN A UNIQUE POSITION TO BE INVOLVED

Mental health professionals play a key role in addressing trauma. So do communities, such as churches, small groups and families. There are practical, illuminating and caring ways for non-professionals to come alongside traumatized people.

A community's acknowledgment and support can make all the difference to people who are suffering. They can take actions that lead to justice for victims. They can prevent similar trauma from happening to others. They can heal together. The benefits of a welcoming network of friends go beyond what any individual can do to help.

American Bible Society believes that churches —who know firsthand the life-changing effects of an encounter with the message of the Bible—have a special opportunity and responsibility to help people heal from trauma. And we are not the only ones who think this way. Most pastors agree that trauma is an issue for the church to address. About two-thirds of Protestant pastors (68%) say churches should be equipped to help congregants with trauma. More than one-third (37%) says the church should extend that care to their neighborhoods and communities, even if those in need are not members of their congregation.

It seems that many outside the church also have this expectation. As this report shows, many people suffering from trauma are open to the church's help, even if they aren't regular churchgoers. Pastors who signal the church's willingness and ability to help tend to see an increase in the number of people who come to them for help with trauma.

Sadly, some people in the church, including church leaders, have *caused* trauma through their actions. Roles that can offer healing can also be manipulated in the hands of ill-equipped and traumatized individuals. Beyond following protocols for allegations of abuse, church leaders will likely be called on to address different forms of trauma in different ways, even among leaders. Churches should be prepared to prevent injury and provide aid so that all may be healed. This begins with understanding and planning for inevitable experiences from the pulpit to the pew.

We believe that the church and the Bible offer hope for healing in Christ. Christians can create an environment for bringing light and relief to those who are suffering. As trauma is woven through the stories of the Bible, from captivity to crucifixion, so, too, is hope. The stories of characters like Tamar and Rahab, Joseph and Paul may well reflect the trauma in the lives of many churchgoers today and the hope that is available in God.

ABS seeks to empower churches to help effectively. Our efforts are coordinated with those of the Trauma Healing Institute, which provides proven

REV. DR. NICOLE MARTIN leads the Trauma Healing enterprise at American Bible Society. She is also an Assistant Professor at Gordon-Conwell Theological Seminary and founder of Soulfire International Ministries. She has published numerous articles in *Christianity Today* and is the author of two books, *Made to Lead: Empowering Women for Ministry* and *Leaning In and Letting Go: A Lenten Devotional*. She serves on the board for the National Association of Evangelicals and on the Board of Trustees at Gordon College. Nicole is a nationally recognized speaker, focusing on engaging all people in the life-changing power of God's Word.

strategies for healing. With the help of an advisory council, the authors behind *Healing the Wounds of Trauma*, the member organizations of Trauma Healing Alliance and its staff, the Trauma Healing Institute produces a series of Bible-based curriculum resources to be used by groups for transformation and hope. You can visit TraumaInAmerica.Bible to learn more about what you can do to heal the wounds of trauma around you.

We hope this study gives hope for healing to those affected by trauma and becomes a starting place for communities and churches who bring light to the suffering.

 **Methodology**

The data reported in this study are based on an online survey of 2,019 adults ages 18 and older in the U.S. who have experienced or witnessed trauma. To qualify for this survey, participants had to have personally experienced a trauma or have witnessed a traumatic event that left them feeling effects or symptoms, such as fear or anxiety, within the past 10 years (even if the traumatic event occurred more than 10 years ago). In this study, 1,015 practicing Christians and 1,004 adults who are not practicing Christians were surveyed (see research definitions for more information on how practicing Christians were defined on page 20). The maximum amount of sample error is plus or minus 1.9 percent at the 95 percent confidence level. The sample error among the practicing Christian sample and the non-practicing Christian sample is plus or minus 2.9 percent at the 95 percent confidence level each.

Additionally, 509 interviews were conducted online with Protestant senior pastors and 60 Catholic priests. Pastors in this database were recruited via probability sampling on annual phone and email surveys, and are representative of U.S. Protestant and Catholic churches by region, denomination and church size. The margin of error for Protestant pastors is plus or minus 4.2 percent at the 95 percent confidence level.

Interviews with adults and senior pastors were conducted from June 6 to June 28, 2019.

In the pastors study, each pastor represents one church, as they are the senior pastor of the church in question. However, the churchgoing respondents are not spread evenly across churches and pastors, so their responses should not be taken as representative of churches but of churchgoers.

Online interviews were conducted using an online research panel. Upon completion of each survey, minimal statistical weights were applied to the data to allow the results to more closely correspond to known national demographic averages for several variables.

When researchers describe the accuracy of survey results, the estimated amount of sampling error is often provided. This refers to the degree of inaccuracy that might be attributable to interviewing a group of people that is not completely representative of the population from which the people were drawn. That estimate is dependent on two factors: (1) the sample size and (2) the degree to which the result being examined is close to 50 percent or the extremes, 0 to 100 percent. Keep in mind that there is a range of other errors that may influence survey results (e.g., biased question wording, question sequencing, inaccurate recording of the responses, inaccurate data tabulation) whose influence cannot be statistically determined.

SAMPLE DIFFERENCES FROM THE POPULATION

This group of traumatized practicing Christians is different from other practicing Christian adults in a couple ways. These differences seem to reflect variations in the lives of those living with trauma, rather than an error in data-gathering.

Marriage

Half of the practicing Christians in this study are married, a lower rate than practicing Christians in general. Marriage is highly linked to age and ethnicity in America. It may also reflect consequences or causes of trauma. The unexpected death of a spouse, for example, results in both trauma and singleness.

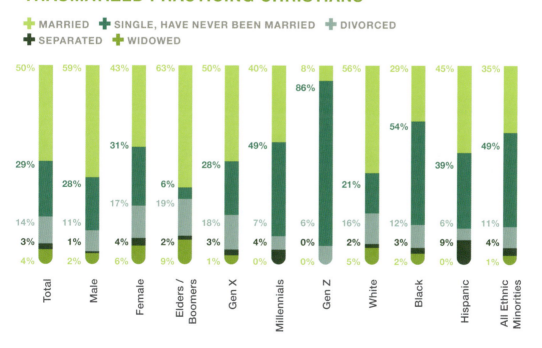

GENDER & AGE GROUP, BY MARITAL STATUS OF TRAUMATIZED PRACTICING CHRISTIANS

✚ MARRIED ✚ SINGLE, HAVE NEVER BEEN MARRIED ✚ DIVORCED
✚ SEPARATED ✚ WIDOWED

n=1,015 practicing Christian adults who experienced trauma; June 6–28, 2019.

Unemployment

There is a high rate of unemployment in this sample, with 46 percent of practicing Christian respondents and 52 percent of others not working for pay. Note that this may be due to retirement (many of these unemployed are of retirement age) or other lifestyle choices, as well as wanting but not having work. Very likely some of these unemployed respondents find that their trauma interferes with their ability to work. Unemployment and salary are, of course, linked. With them is tied the financial advantage of marriage; a dual-income family is likely more financially resilient.

GLOSSARY

Destitution	not having enough food, clothing or shelter
Vigilance	always on alert or on guard; feeling jumpy
Rumination	replaying or reliving the event over and over in your mind
Practicing Christians	identify as Christian, confirm they have been to a regular church service in the past month and agree strongly that "my religious faith is very important in my life"

 **Chapter One**

INCIDENCE OF TRAUMA

One in five U.S adults has experienced the effects of trauma in the past 10 years. This rate is similar inside and outside of the church, with 20 percent of practicing Christians and 19 percent of other U.S. adults reporting a traumatic experience.

How did the researchers determine these one in five adults as being impacted by trauma?

✚ When asked, "Have you ever experienced physical, psychological or emotional trauma, such as extreme violence, abuse or a near-death experience that produces a response of intense fear, helplessness or horror lasting more than a few weeks?" respondents selected:
  ✗ "You personally experienced a trauma"
  ✗ "You witnessed a trauma involving an immediate family member" and / or

One in five U.S adults has experienced the effects of trauma in the past 10 years

- ✕ "You witnessed a trauma involving someone other than a family member"
- ✚ When asked, "Have you experienced any impacts, effects or symptoms related to trauma, such as fear or anxiety, within the past 10 years, even if the traumatic event occurred more than 10 years ago?" respondents selected, "Yes."

Some groups are more likely to report experiencing trauma. For instance, women seem to have a much higher incidence of trauma than men. Millennials are much more likely than Boomers to report trauma, while Gen X falls between. White and Asian Americans report lower incidence of trauma than black Americans and Hispanic Americans. College graduates report a lower incidence of trauma than those with less formal education.

Unfortunately, those who have experienced trauma are often re-traumatized both in the severity of the event and by the subsequent symptoms these groups report, given that victims reported having experienced something that produced a response of intense fear, helplessness or horror lasting more than a few weeks.

Pastors also had the opportunity to share about their personal encounters with trauma in a separate survey. Exactly four in 10 say they experienced trauma because of something that happened to them; 35 percent say they experienced trauma because of something that happened to a family member; 38 percent say they experienced trauma because of something that happened to someone other than a family member and 36 percent say they have not had any of those experiences.

THE SYMPTOMS & SEVERITY OF TRAUMA'S IMPACT

Sleep disturbances (52%), ruminating on the traumatic event (49%) and anxiety (49%) are the most common symptoms among practicing

SYMPTOMS OF TRAUMA AMONG PRACTICING CHRISTIANS

OFTEN   OCCASIONALLY   RARELY   NEVER

Symptom	Often	Occasionally	Rarely	Never
Sleep disturbances / nightmares about the event	27%	21%	4%	48%
Becoming very anxious when something reminds you of the event	27%	20%	2%	51%
Replaying or reliving the event over and over in your mind	25%	20%	5%	51%
Avoiding thoughts or memories related to the trauma	25%	15%	1%	59%
Grief or a sense of loss	23%	18%	4%	56%
Avoiding reminders of the event (avoiding places, people, activities, etc.)	21%	17%	3%	59%
Having strong negative feelings such as anger, fear, horror	20%	18%	4%	58%
Always on alert or on guard; feeling jumpy	20%	17%	2%	61%
Loss of interest in activities you used to enjoy	20%	17%	2%	61%
Shame or guilt	20%	14%	4%	68%
Feeling like no one is listening to you / you've lost your voice	20%	10%	2%	68%
Withdrawing from family or friends	18%	16%	3%	63%
A feeling of helplessness that lasted more than just a few weeks	17%	16%	4%	63%
Trouble experiencing feelings (unable to feel happiness / love)	16%	14%	3%	67%
Unable to eat or overeating	15%	13%	4%	68%
Irritable behavior, angry outbursts or aggressive behavior	15%	12%	4%	69%
Experiencing physical symptoms when thinking about the event	13%	17%	5%	65%
Negative behaviors (alcohol / substance abuse, self harm, etc.)	11%	9%	4%	76%

n=1,007 practicing Christian adults who experienced trauma; June 6–28, 2019.

SYMPTOMS OF TRAUMA AMONG NON-PRACTICING CHRISTIANS & NON-CHRISTIANS

+ OFTEN   + OCCASIONALLY   + RARELY   + NEVER

Symptom	Often	Occasionally	Rarely	Never
Sleep disturbances / nightmares about the event	32%	17%	4%	46%
Becoming very anxious when something reminds you of the event	32%	17%	3%	48%
Always on alert or on guard; feeling jumpy	27%	13%	1%	59%
Avoiding thoughts or memories related to the trauma	26%	17%	2%	54%
Loss of interest in activities you used to enjoy	25%	14%	3%	57%
Withdrawing from family or friends	24%	16%	4%	56%
Having strong negative feelings such as anger, fear, horror	23%	21%	4%	53%
Grief or a sense of loss	23%	19%	5%	54%
Feeling like no one is listening to you / you've lost your voice	23%	11%	1%	65%
Replaying or reliving the event over and over in your mind	22%	19%	3%	56%
Avoiding reminders of the event (avoiding places, people, activities, etc.)	22%	16%	2%	60%
A feeling of helplessness that lasted more than just a few weeks	20%	14%	5%	61%
Shame or guilt	18%	14%	2%	65%
Unable to eat or overeating	18%	14%	3%	64%
Trouble experiencing feelings (unable to feel happiness / love)	17%	14%	4%	65%
Experiencing physical symptoms when thinking about the event	16%	17%	4%	62%
Irritable behavior, angry outbursts or aggressive behavior	16%	15%	5%	64%
Negative behaviors (alcohol / substance abuse, self harm, etc.)	15%	9%	4%	73%

n=997 non-practicing Christian and non-Christian adults who experienced trauma; June 6–28, 2019.

Christians who have been traumatized. About half of practicing Christians with trauma experience these symptoms. These are similar to the top symptoms among non-practicing Christians and non-Christians, with sleep disturbances (54%) and anxiety (52%) being most common, though this group is less likely to report ruminations (44%).

About a quarter of practicing Christians who have been impacted by trauma says they "often" experience these symptoms. Similar proportions frequently experience grief (23%), strong negative feelings (20%), avoiding reminders of the event (21%), vigilance (20%), loss of interest in activities they used to enjoy (20%), shame or guilt (20%) or withdrawal from loved ones (18%).

About one-third of traumatized practicing Christians reports any incidence of changes in how they eat (33%), aggressive or irritable behavior (32%) or self-destructive behaviors like substance abuse or self-harm (25%). Statistically, non-practicing Christians and non-Christians are more likely than practicing Christians to experience aggressive or irritable behavior (36%), while disruption to eating habits (36%) and negative behaviors (28%) show little to no significant difference.

TYPES OF TRAUMATIC EXPERIENCES

Two-fifths of practicing Christians (40%) say their trauma was incited by the death of a loved one, the most common cause among this group. The next most commonly mentioned cause of trauma was betrayal by a trusted individual, noted by one-third of the group (33%). Forms of abuse such as domestic violence (27%), physical abuse (22%) and sexual abuse (21%) follow in frequency. Few practicing Christians say they've been traumatized by homicide or suicide, although suicide remains a leading cause of death.[2]

The rates of traumatic events vary by faith segment, with non-Christians being more likely than practicing Christians to say

TRAUMATIC EVENTS

PRACTICING CHRISTIANS   NON-PRACTICING CHRISTIANS   NON-CHRISTIANS

Event	Practicing Christians	Non-Practicing Christians	Non-Christians
Death of a loved one	40%	42%	43%
Betrayal by someone you trusted	33%	37%	38%
Domestic violence	27%	28%	37%
Physical abuse	22%	22%	34%
Sexual abuse	21%	20%	28%
Watching someone die or being abused	19%	21%	27%
Near death experience or signficant injury	17%	18%	24%
Major financial setback	16%	20%	20%
Job loss	16%	19%	19%
Divorce	14%	14%	16%
Addiction	12%	18%	17%
Not having enough food	11%	21%	22%
Child abuse	11%	13%	20%
Suicide	9%	13%	16%
Prison	7%	8%	9%
Conflicts, such as wars	7%	5%	10%
Natural disasters	7%	4%	5%
Burglary / robbery	6%	6%	9%
Exposed to trauma through job	5%	6%	6%
Racial discrimination	5%	4%	8%
Homicide	3%	4%	3%

n=1,992 adults who experienced trauma; June 6–28, 2019.

they have been traumatized by most of the events listed. This is particularly striking when looking at reports of physical abuse (34% vs. 22%), destitution (22% vs. 11%), domestic violence (37% vs. 27%), child abuse (20% vs. 11%) or witnessing the death or abuse of someone else (27% vs. 19%). Between non-practicing and practicing Christians, there is also a significant difference in experiences of destitution (21% vs. 11%) and addiction (18% vs. 12%).

This information does not tell us the precise timing of when people experience trauma and whether a respondent was a part of a church when the traumatizing incident occurred. However, it can indicate to church leaders what people inside or outside the church may be dealing with now. At this rate, we can assume that in an average 10-person small group, two will have experienced trauma. In a 200-person congregation, on average, 40 will have experienced trauma (and just under half of them are likely to have experienced domestic, physical or sexual abuse). In a megachurch, this rises into the hundreds. Trauma may not be evenly spread across churches, and some may have a heavier burden of trauma than others.

Outside church contexts, in a 200-person group at, say, a wedding or a mid-sized business, about 38 people will have experienced trauma in the past 10 years, and about 19 will have experienced domestic abuse. Five are likely to have been affected by someone's suicide.

A COMPOUNDED IMPACT: COMBINATIONS OF SYMPTOMS & EVENTS

Even fairly rare traumatic events have effects on multiple people that can last over long periods of time, accumulating an impact that extends far beyond the individual who personally experienced an incident and the period when it occurred. Some symptoms and events may also overlap, as the following pages and tables detail.

We can assume that in a 10-person small group, two will have experienced trauma

PAIRS OF SYMPTOMS

Sleep disturbances are the most likely to pair at a high rate with other symptoms. Anxiety also surfaces alongside other symptoms.

Among those who experience sleep disturbances, three-quarters of practicing Christians (73%) and others (75%) also experience irritable or aggressive behavior. Similarly, three-quarters of all respondents (77% of practicing Christians, 75% of others) who experience diet disturbances also experience sleep disturbances. Practicing Christians who have faced a feeling of helplessness that lasted more than just a few weeks are highly likely to also experience sleep disturbances (73%).

Three-quarters of practicing Christians who experience physical symptoms (77%) or irritable or aggressive behavior (74%) also sense anxiety when reminded about the traumatic event. A similar proportion of non-practicing Christians and non-Christians who report avoiding reminders of the event (76%) report becoming very anxious when memories do surface.

Four in 10 non-practicing Christians and non-Christians who report loss of interest in activities they used to enjoy also engage in negative behaviors like substance abuse or self-harm (42%). This is also on par with practicing Christians' tendencies, as nearly two in five (39%) said the same.

PAIRS OF EVENTS & SYMPTOMS

There is no symptom that *always* accompanies a particular traumatic event. This may have to do with the timeline of events and other factors in individual cases. However, some symptoms are fairly typical after traumatizing incidents. More than four in 10 non-practicing Christians and non-Christians who experience any traumatic event also experience grief or a sense of loss (46%), anxiety (52%) and avoiding thoughts or memories of the event (40%). Many other symptoms also accompany at least half the traumatic events listed.

The most frequent pairing of a type of trauma and a type of symptom occurs among practicing Christians who have faced destitution, a majority of whom selects *all* of the possible symptoms. Roughly three-quarters of those who have experienced not having enough food, clothing or shelter say they have become very anxious when something reminds them of this trauma (76%), withdrawn from family or friends (73%), experienced sleep disturbances (72%), felt like no one was listening to them or like they didn't have a voice (72%), become vigilant (71%) or replayed or relived the traumatic event (70%). Clearly, destitution has a deep, lasting impact and we can assume many who report this type of personal trauma may have also experienced homelessness, displacement or other life-altering forms of deprivation.

Three of four non-practicing Christians and non-Christians who have been exposed to details about others' trauma through their jobs also experience sleep disturbances (76%).

PAIRS OF TRAUMATIC EVENTS

Trauma is rarely a one-time occurance. There is somewhat less overlap in traumatizing incidents among practicing Christians compared to other respondents, but a minority of traumatized people (31% of practicing Christians, 27% of non-practicing Christians and non-Christians) reports facing only a single traumatic event. Still, as with combinations of symptoms, there are no traumatic events that *always* coexist.

Among practicing Christians, the death of a loved one is the most commonly experienced trauma. Those who have experienced the death of a loved one are more likely to have also experienced a sense of betrayal by a loved one (42% vs. 33% on average), domestic violence (34% vs. 27%), watching someone die or be abused (33% vs. 19%), physical abuse (30% vs. 22%), sexual abuse (26% vs. 21%) or addiction (18% vs. 12%).

A sense of betrayal is likewise common among people who have dealt with trauma from destitution (62% of practicing Christians, 67%

A minority of traumatized people reports facing only a single traumatic event

PRACTICING CHRISTIANS: OVERLAP OF CAUSES OF TRAUMA

✚ HIGH OVERLAP   ✚ MODERATE OVERLAP   ✚ LOW OVERLAP   ✚ NO OVERLAP

% WHO HAVE EXPERIENCED...*
...HAVE ALSO EXPERIENCED:

	Not having enough food, clothing or shelter	Child abuse	Major financial setback (i.e., home foreclosure, bankruptcy)	Divorce	Physical abuse	Addiction
Divorce	24%	22%	27%		23%	
Destitution		25%	31%	19%	27%	33%
Physical abuse	52%	60%	34%	35%		37%
Addiction	36%				21%	
Domestic violence, including verbal abuse	62%	65%	47%	50%	64%	45%
Job loss			36%	34%		39%
Conflicts such as wars, bombings or other types of attacks	15%		14%			
Sexual abuse or unwanted sexual contact	43%	60%	33%	30%	47%	
Watching someone die or being abused	33%	35%	30%	33%		28%
Homicide						
Betrayal by a loved one or someone you trusted	62%	61%	56%	67%	57%	50%
Repeatedly exposed to details about trauma on job	13%	9%	11%	13%	8%	
Near death experience or significant injury	26%		28%	27%		
Death of a loved one	70%	51%	62%	51%	55%	57%
Natural disasters	13%					14%
Racial discrimination	10%	12%		14%	10%	
Burglary / robbery	18%	19%	11%	13%	14%	12%
Major financial setback	43%	26%		31%	25%	
Prison / incarceration	18%	12%			14%	24%
Suicide	17%	16%	14%	19%	17%	17%

TRAUMA IN AMERICA

This chart does not show significant difference among overlapping causes, merely the percentage at which respondents report overlap occurring.

Domestic violence, including verbal abuse	Job loss	Sexual abuse or unwanted sexual contact	Watching someone die or being abused	Betrayal by a loved one or someone you trusted	Near death experience or significant injury, such as from an accident or shooting	Death of a loved one
26%	29%	19%	25%	28%	21%	18%
26%	26%	23%		21%		20%
52%		48%		37%		30%
			18%	19%		18%
44%	35%	48%	34%	47%		34%
39%	29%			23%	27%	
12%						
37%				37%		26%
	28%			28%		33%
			6%			
57%	47%	57%	49%		39%	42%
8%	12%	8%	11%			
	28%					
57%	55%		69%	51%		
15%	14%					
	13%		13%	10%		
13%	11%	10%		11%		
28%	35%	25%	26%	27%	26%	25%
10%	23%	14%	14%	11%		10%
18%		15%		13%		

*Due to lower sample size among those who have experienced natural disasters, conflicts such as wars, bombings or other types of attacks, racial discrimination, burglary / robbery, repeated exposure to details about trauma at their job, prison / incarceration, homicide or suicide, we cannot report on their experiences with other types of trauma, though overlap does occur.

n=1,013 practicing Christian adults who experienced trauma; June 6–28, 2019.

of others), child abuse (61% vs. 59%), a major financial setback (56% vs. 63%), divorce (67% vs. 65%), physical abuse (57% vs. 60%), addiction (50% vs. 57%), domestic violence (57% vs. 65%) and sexual abuse (57% vs. 58%).

Although less common, domestic abuse frequently accompanies physical abuse (52% of practicing Christians vs. 55% of others), destitution (26% vs. 40%), child abuse (25% vs. 37%) and divorce (26% each).

Child abuse is seldom isolated from other trauma. Only 2 percent of practicing Christians and 8 percent of others say they experienced child abuse as a single traumatizing event. Usually, those traumatized by child abuse have also dealt with physical abuse (60% of practicing Christians, 68% of others), domestic violence (65% vs. 66%), sexual abuse (60% vs. 57%), betrayal by someone they trusted (61% vs. 59%) and the death of a loved one (51% vs. 48%).

Pastors should expect to deal with an array of traumatic events and symptoms. For example, if they feel able to deal with domestic violence but not child abuse, they may be less able to help the many individuals who suffer from both.

RECENCY OF TRAUMA

Most respondents in this study do not report experiencing ongoing trauma. Keep in mind that the sample is of people who agree that they have experienced "impacts, effects or symptoms related to trauma, such as fear or anxiety, within the past 10 years, even if the traumatic event occurred more than 10 years ago."

Seven in 10 practicing Christians (70%) say they experienced the traumatic event in the past, two in 10 (18%) say they experienced it recently, and one in 10 (12%) is currently navigating a traumatic event.

In the non-practicing Christian and non-Christian samples, the ratios are similar. Non-practicing Christians and non-Christians are slightly more likely to say their traumatic event is in the past (76%). One in seven non-practicing Christians and non-Christians (14%) says they've experienced trauma recently, and one in 10 (10%) says they are currently experiencing something traumatic.

Protestant pastors who have witnessed or experienced traumatizing events are more likely to have done so in the past (87%) and less likely to be currently experiencing something traumatic (2%).

ARE YOU CURRENTLY EXPERIENCING TRAUMA, OR DID THIS HAPPEN IN THE PAST?

✚ PASTORS ✚ PRACTICING CHRISTIANS
✚ NON-PRACTICING CHRISTIANS ✚ NON-CHRISTIANS

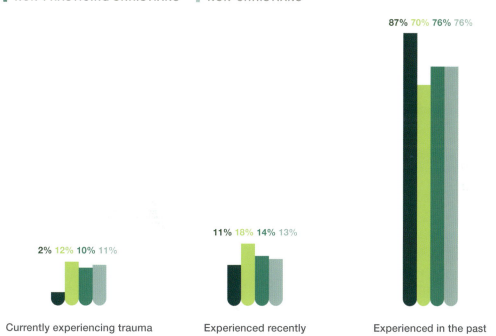

Currently experiencing trauma: 2% 12% 10% 11%
Experienced recently: 11% 18% 14% 13%
Experienced in the past: 87% 70% 76% 76%

n=2,019 adults who experienced trauma; June 6–28, 2019.

INCIDENCE OF TRAUMA | 33

HOW TRAUMATIZED PRACTICING CHRISTIANS THINK ABOUT & USE THE BIBLE

Practicing Christians who have experienced trauma skew more toward the extremes of Scripture engagement—in other words, they are more Bible-centered, tending to turn to the Bible more, or more Bible-disengaged, tending to turn to the Bible less, than practicing Christians generally. It is possible practicing Christians have either found comfort from their trauma in the Bible or they have not and are struggling to engage with Scripture.

Most traumatized practicing Christians say they use the Bible several times a week or more,

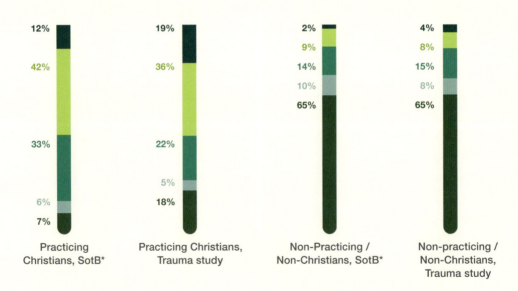

COMPARING BIBLE ENGAGEMENT SEGMENTS AMONG PRACTICING CHRISTIANS

COMPARING BIBLE ENGAGEMENT SEGMENTS AMONG NON-PRACTICING CHRISTIANS

✚ CENTERED ✚ ENGAGED ✚ FRIENDLY ✚ NEUTRAL ✚ DISENGAGED

	Practicing Christians, SotB*	Practicing Christians, Trauma study	Non-Practicing / Non-Christians, SotB*	Non-practicing / Non-Christians, Trauma study
Disengaged (top)	12%	19%	2%	4%
Neutral	42%	36%	9%	8%
Friendly			14%	15%
Engaged	33%	22%	10%	8%
Centered (bottom)	6% / 7%	5% / 18%	65%	65%

*To see how trauma sufferers' Bible engagement compares to that of the general population, the distribution of Bible engagement segments was compared to the ABS State of the Bible (SotB) study, an annual study of U.S. adults and their perceptions and use of the Bible.
n=2,019 U.S. adults who experienced trauma, June 6–28, 2019.
n=2,013 U.S. adults, *State of the Bible* Study, January 15–February 7, 2019.

TRAUMATIZED PRACTICING CHRISTIANS: FREQUENCY OF BIBLE USE

TRAUMATIZED NON-PRACTICING & NON-CHRISTIANS: FREQUENCY OF BIBLE USE

✚ EVERY DAY ✚ FOUR OR MORE TIMES A WEEK ✚ SEVERAL TIMES A WEEK
✚ ONCE A WEEK ✚ ONCE A MONTH ✚ THREE OR FOUR TIMES A YEAR
✚ ONCE OR TWICE A YEAR ✚ LESS THAN ONCE A YEAR ✚ NEVER

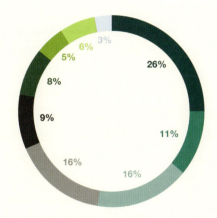

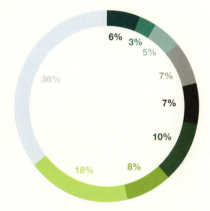

n=988 practicing Christian adults who experienced trauma; June 6–28, 2019.

n=980 non-practicing Christian and non-Christian adults who experienced trauma; June 6–28, 2019.

whether generally (53%) or on their own (59%). One-quarter (26%) uses the Bible every day.

As one might expect, Bible engagement is less common among those who are not practicing Christians. However, only about one-third (36%) says they never read the Bible. One in seven (14%) says they use the Bible more than once a week.

Looking more closely at faith segments, about one-fifth of non-practicing but self-identified Christians never reads the Bible (22%)—similar to the proportion who reads it multiple times each week (19%). Six in 10 non-Christians (58%), meanwhile, never read the Bible. Within that group of non-Christians, those who affiliate with other religions are, unsurprisingly, less likely to read the Bible than those with no religion (67% vs. 50% never read the Bible).

While Christians may overreport their Bible use thinking it's the "correct" thing to do, the data suggest many traumatized people both inside and outside the church encounter the Bible frequently, with most engaging with it at least sometimes.

DEGREE OF TRAUMA

While the incidence of trauma in this study—about one-fifth—indicates how widespread the experience is inside and outside of the church, it is also important to recognize the degree to which people are impacted by traumatic events. Understanding what factors affect a person's degree of trauma can help give perspective on what their needs may be and how to best minister to them.

Multiple factors make a difference in how people rate their level of trauma: education, age, marriage, employment, recency of the trauma and how well they believe they're coping with their trauma. Respondents were asked to rank their trauma from zero to 10, where 10 was overwhelming and five was moderate.

Faith segments experience similar degrees of trauma. About half of respondents (48% of practicing Christians and others, respectively) put themselves in middle categories, rating the severity of their trauma from five to seven. Just over one-quarter of each group (practicing Christians and others) puts themselves in the higher category, eight to 10, and an equal one-quarter rates the trauma as zero to four.

What distinguishes the degree of trauma a person will experience? Looking at factors a person cannot or cannot easily change, the biggest influence on the severity of a person's trauma is how recently they experienced the traumatic event (ongoing, recent or in the past). The more recent a traumatic event, the more overwhelming it is to a respondent. To untangle relationships among other personal characteristics and identify those that most influence the severity of trauma, researchers conducted a regression analysis that allowed them to consider multiple factors at once.

Narrowing the key demographic factors down to education, age, marital status and employment and equalizing the influence of time (recency), researchers found that each of these characteristics had a reliable effect on how severe a person's trauma was. That is, the

The more recent a traumatic event was, the more overwhelming it is to a respondent

degree of trauma people experience can be partially accounted for by a combination of their education, age, how recently they had experienced trauma, whether they are married and their employment status.

How do these factors correlate with trauma impact? Researchers found that, when other factors, including marriage, are accounted for, a lower degree of trauma is correlated with higher educational attainment, greater age, working part-time and a greater length of time having elapsed since a traumatic event. Thus, a person who is old, well-educated, employed and whose traumatic event is in the past is likely to experience a lesser degree of trauma than someone without those characteristics. (This is not the same as *coping well* with trauma, which will be covered later in this report).

GROUPS THAT EXPERIENCE TRAUMA DIFFERENTLY

GENERATION / AGE

Generational differences, among both practicing Christians and others, influence how respondents answered a high proportion of the questions about trauma. In general, older Americans report less intense trauma, though other research on this generation suggests they may downplay their experiences or symptoms. This is true among both practicing Christians and other respondents.

LOCATION

Traumatized Americans are geographically evenly distributed. This sample lives in neighborhoods that closely match data from the U.S. Department of Housing and Urban Development's 2017 American Housing Survey's Neighborhood Description Survey (which, however, did not have "small town" as an option[3]). Given this close match, there does not seem to be a difference in the proportion of traumatized people by neighborhood type.

GENDER

Women, both practicing Christian and non-practicing / non-Christian, are more likely than men to report that the death of a loved one, betrayal, domestic violence, physical abuse, child abuse, sexual abuse or destitution traumatized them.

Traumatized practicing Christian men are more likely than women to report trauma through a near-death experience, incarceration, job

TRAUMATIC EVENTS, BY RELIGION & GENDER

+ PRACTICING CHRISTIAN MEN   + NON-PRACTICING / NON-CHRISTIAN MEN
+ PRACTICING CHRISTIAN WOMEN + NON-PRACTICING / NON-CHRISTIAN WOMEN

Event	PC Men	NP/NC Men	PC Women	NP/NC Women
Death of a loved one	32%	38%	45%	45%
Near death experience or significant injury	23%	23%	13%	18%
Betrayal by someone you trusted	21%	28%	42%	44%
Job loss	20%	21%	13%	17%
Domestic violence, including verbal abuse	19%	17%	32%	42%
Physical abuse	16%	19%	26%	33%
Child abuse	5%	12%	14%	19%
Prison / incarceration	10%	10%	5%	7%
Sexual abuse or unwanted sexual contact	8%	12%	31%	32%
Not having enough food, clothing or shelter	8%	19%	13%	24%

n=2,013 adults who experienced trauma; June 6–28, 2019.

loss and conflicts such as wars, bombing and other attacks, while non-practicing Christian men are more likely than women to report trauma through conflict, such as wars, bombings or other types of attacks.

Another difference is the degree to which men and women experience different symptoms. Women report experiencing *all* listed symptoms at an equal or higher rate than men, among both practicing Christians and others.

EDUCATION, INCOME & SOCIOECONOMIC STATUS

There are many differences in how people experience trauma according to their education, and education is closely linked to salary and socioeconomic status. While the rate of college degrees in the United States has been rising for several generations, only one-third of U.S. adults has a bachelor's degree or higher, according to the U.S. Census Bureau.[4]

A college education may signal other elements of a person's background, including family wealth, social support or having dependents in early adulthood, as well as elements of that person's present circumstances (income and type of work) or personal characteristics (such as grit or ability to focus) that may have been affected by trauma or the person's ability to deal with it. That is to say, a college degree does not seem to be a *cause* of less trauma, but there are good reasons to expect a strong correlation between more education and less trauma.

College-educated traumatized practicing Christians are less likely than all others to have experienced domestic violence (18% vs. 31% of others) or physical abuse (14% vs. 25%). They are also less likely than those with a high school education or less to have encountered addiction (8% vs. 13%), sexual abuse (16% vs. 23%), death of a loved one (30% vs. 46%) and not having enough food or other essentials (7% vs. 13%). Many of these correspond to known symptoms of poverty.

While this study does not show causal flow—we cannot answer which came first, which causes the other or whether there is another element we don't see—those who are less educated are more likely to experience many of the symptoms asked about.

In particular, practicing Christians with a high school education are more likely than college-educated practicing Christians to avoid reminders of the event, by 23 percentage points (53% vs. 30%). They are also more likely to experience strong negative feelings (51% vs. 36%), becoming very anxious when something reminds them of the event (56% vs. 41%), negative behaviors (30% vs. 16%), feeling like no one is listening to them or that they have lost their voice (40% vs. 27%), shame or guilt (45% vs. 32%) and avoiding thoughts or memories related to the trauma (49% vs. 36%).

Non-practicing Christians and non-Christians also have different experiences with trauma according to their education level. College graduates are less likely than those with a high school education to have faced traumatic events such as domestic violence (22% vs. 32%), addiction (13% vs. 20%), physical abuse (16% vs. 31%), sexual abuse (14% vs. 24%), child abuse (9% vs. 19%) and destitution (7% vs. 27%). People with a high school education are more likely than those with a college education to say they've experienced having strong negative feelings such as anger, fear or horror (49% vs. 40%) or that they felt unheard (40% vs. 25%).

Neither practicing Christians nor non-practicing / non-Christian college graduates are more likely than those without a college education to have sought out help for their trauma.

These differences in education, in combination, point to a vulnerable group: Those without a college education are more likely to suffer from certain traumatic events and simultaneously to have strong emotional reactions, including guilt, a sense of being unable to express themselves and an impulse to avoid the topic. Those in churches might consider how to ease the burdens of traumatized people with less education, perhaps by deliberately providing the sort of social safety net most college graduates enjoy. This might reduce the chance that people in this category would have a lower rate of seeking out help.

SYMPTOMS OF TRAUMA AMONG PRACTICING CHRISTIANS, BY EDUCATION LEVEL

✚ HIGH SCHOOL OR LESS ✚ SOME COLLEGE ✚ COLLEGE GRADUATE

Symptom	High school or less	Some college	College graduate
Sleep disturbances / nightmares about event	56%	52%	47%
Becoming very anxious when something reminds you of the event	56%	54%	41%
Replaying or reliving the event over and over in your mind	55%	48%	46%
Avoiding reminders of the event (avoiding places, people, activities, etc.)	53%	38%	30%
Having strong negative feelings such as anger, fear, horror	51%	38%	36%
Avoiding thoughts or memories related to the trauma	49%	42%	36%
Shame or guilt	45%	37%	32%
Grief or a sense of loss	44%	53%	39%
Always on alert or on guard; feeling jumpy	43%	40%	37%
Loss of interest in activities you used to enjoy	43%	47%	31%
Withdrawing from family or friends	42%	41%	32%
A feeling of helplessness that lasted more than just a few weeks	42%	40%	31%
Feeling like no one is listening to you / you've lost your voice	40%	30%	27%
Experiencing physical symptoms when thinking about the event	39%	35%	30%
Unable to eat or overeating	36%	34%	28%
Trouble experiencing feelings (unable to feel happiness / love)	33%	36%	30%
Irritable behavior, angry outbursts or aggressive behavior	33%	34%	28%
Negative behaviors (alcohol / substance abuse, self harm, etc.)	30%	28%	16%

n=1,007 practicing Christian adults who experienced trauma; June 6–28, 2019.

WHEN TRAUMA BECOMES NORMAL
BY NICOLE MARTIN

The State of the Bible research reveals African Americans as the most Bible-engaged demographic in the United States for the past 10 years. This finding resonates with my family stories. My great-grandmother fought to desegregate schools in Pittsburgh in the 1960s and read the Bible every day. Her parents struggled through economic hardship but built a church so black families could have a sacred space to encounter God in the projects where they lived. Their ability to overcome hardship with the strength of God's Word demonstrates how easy it is for some racial and ethnic groups to accept trauma as a normal part of life, leaning on God to survive.

This idea of normalizing racial trauma as part of lived experience is complex. On one hand, those who live through systematic and personal oppression can develop callouses that keep us from feeling everyday pain. My parents, who had to stand against Jim Crow, are less likely to complain about not being heard or feeling judged. At times, generational trauma teaches us to accept and learn to rise above pain to keep going.

On the other hand, the experience of trauma among people of color can make most of life feel traumatic. The saying, "if it's not one thing, it's another," hits home as personal suffering intersects with societal injustice. Some feel like they're constantly fighting against evil and become weary from the effort to live healthy lives. The extremes of normalizing trauma and over-emphasizing trauma are both valid experiences that must be held in tandem to open our hearts to a fuller understanding of God's healing and grace.

In communities like mine, knowing Jesus said we would experience trouble in the world strengthens us when we must simply move forward. Understanding the importance of biblical justice can be a means of grace when we need to persevere. These complexities are best unpacked in community with others who can sympathize, hear, and at least try to understand.

No single response will heal all wounds of racial trauma, but community plays one of the most significant roles. Experiencing Christ in community with others can make space for lament and give us words to articulate how we feel. I have seen the truest forms of racial solidarity usher in the healing of Jesus and draw people closer to Christ and each other. I have seen healing show up in my life when friends and colleagues across racial lines take time to understand the complexity of my trauma. In such communities, there is no need to rush to solutions. Sometimes, simply taking the step to understand someone else's path is the best and most important thing we can do continue God's complex and comprehensive healing work.

(See bio on page 15.)

RACE & ETHNICITY

Ethnicity plays a significant role in how we perceive stress, trauma and loss. Issues including racism, socioeconomic barriers, health disparities and more can impact the way families and individuals navigate life. This is especially true for black and Hispanic Americans often disproportionately affected by pandemics, including COVID-19. Such families are faced with unusual amounts of stress and loss which can provoke trauma for many generations.

Fortunately, strong community, high trends of Scripture engagement and church involvement often provide anchors to counterbalance the challenges that ethnic communities may face.

In this study, minorities are more likely than white respondents to say they have witnessed trauma and that this trauma is ongoing and severe. However, white adults are actually more likely to report having had a personal experience of trauma (typically in the past) and more likely to identify with certain incidents and symptoms of trauma suggested in the survey.

It is important to emphasize here that this study was designed to look at trauma, but it did not include a deep investigation of racial or generational trauma. The seeming dissonance of minorities reporting high rates of trauma yet being less likely to attach themselves to particular events or symptoms reveals a need for further research. It is possible that some of the sources of trauma listed are simply more likely to be issues for the majority culture, while minorities might be more represented among survivors of unlisted traumatic events such as community violence, internalized racism, lack of employment opportunities, bullying, microaggressions or other effects of racism or systemic poverty.

Other studies back up this hypothesis, pointing to the high levels of violence, stigma and financial barriers facing many non-white communities and which persist over multiple generations.[5] Additionally, some researchers theorize not only that white adults over-report trauma but also that minorities may rate lower in their experience of mental health problems because they see their hardships as a norm, or even something to reframe in a positive light.[6] Meanwhile, awareness and support for trauma recovery may not be as accessible among minority populations in the United States; consider, for example, that in this Barna study white respondents are less likely than black respondents to say no one was listening to them in the wake of trauma.

Church leaders will find it important to be educated about racial and generational trauma and about the gravity of its effects on people within their communities and congregations. Predominantly white congregations can use personal trauma as a way of connecting with the stories of others who face communal trauma. In this way, personal pain can be a catalyst to learn from and stand in solidarity with others who experience pain. Non-white Christians have much to teach about resilience and reliance on their faith and community through ongoing trauma or post-trauma reactions linked to systemic injustice. Questions raised from these experiences also shape the way communities encounter the Bible, frequently illuminating the text and enriching the levels at which people encounter its message.

Congregations of color can lean into collective trauma as a means of experiencing the fullness of God's healing. Making room for grief and lament at the cross can lead to the joy of resurrection. Church leaders serving these demographics can also benefit from partners across racial and ethnic lines to expand the narrative of suffering into one of unified faith and strength.

> **Church leaders will find it important to be educated about racial and generational trauma**

FACTORS AFFECTING TRAUMA SYMPTOMS
BY HARRIET HILL

SPIRALS OF LOSS

One stress researcher describes "loss spirals" that increase the effects of trauma for those with fewer resources.[7] The process goes like this:

1. Trauma results in loss of resources, both material and immaterial.
2. Resilient individuals are better able to use their remaining resources.
3. It costs money and resources to be resilient.
4. People lose social and economic capital with each trauma, so they have fewer resources and are forced to take more risky strategies to survive.
5. People are less able to cope with each trauma. Trauma begets trauma.
6. Families who suffer generational trauma inherit fewer resources. Well-being becomes something they have to work hard to achieve.

Those with more resources may not be fully protected from trauma, but often have a better chance of recovering. However, significant trauma has a long shelf life, and is sometimes kept for a lifetime, under the surface, nefariously affecting the person's well-being.

SCRIPTURE & COMMUNITY

Research suggests that some expressions of faith can reduce the effects of trauma and increase healthy coping skills. While this is true, the nature of the faith matters. If people believe that God has abandoned them or is punishing them for their sins, it is likely to make their recovery from trauma more difficult. If they believe God may be strengthening them through the situation, it is likely to help them recover from trauma.

Trauma isolates. Shame isolates. To heal from trauma, we need to be in relationship with others. Even our minds are created to live in community. A child who does not attach to at least one adult will have serious emotional problems.

When we are known by others, we have joy and are curious and creative. We know ourselves as we are known by others. Often, this reciprocal relationship of knowing and being known—especially in our pain—is one of the ways we come to experience God. And to know God, we have to know ourselves. We were made to need each other as we grow in connection to God (see, for example, Ephesians 4:12–13). The church's role is to be a healing community.

(See bio on page 62.)

HOW THE PRESENCE OF HOPE AIDS HEALING

A Q&A WITH CHAN HELLMAN

Q: What led you into studying hope?

A: After I finished my PhD work in quantitative psychology, I came to the University of Oklahoma where my primary responsibility as a professor was to teach research methods in a department that provides training for people pursuing a license in professional counseling.

During this time, I met a young man—just turned 19—who had recently been diagnosed with HIV and was also newly homeless. Yet he wasn't depressed, anxious, fearful or socially isolated. He was very engaged.

He introduced me to the concept of hope. He didn't use that word specifically, but he was talking about his goals of going to college and identifying very specific pathways to achieve that goal. That really struck me.

All of my work on hope is in the context of despair and trauma. I come from a background of pretty high trauma myself; I was homeless from seventh grade and throughout high school.

A big part of my research also has to do with me trying to figure out my own journey. For example, why am I resilient but my sibling really struggles? From my perspective, it's hope. I'm completely convinced that hope is a social gift.

Q: Can you expound on that?

A: I am convinced that hope does not operate in isolation. Hope is something that is built upon relationships. Through this, we overcome the guilt and shame of our own experience.

Is it something that comes from our heart? Or our head? Is it outside of us? I am really wrestling with the connection between religiosity, or spirituality, and hope.

But I think hope is a thought process—a way of thinking—and as best as I can tell so far, I think that our conviction in religion or spirituality is the moral compass that guides our hope.

Q: Does hope buffer trauma?

A: We've seen that with people who have a high level of trauma, nurturing their hope does help buffer the adversity and stress. For instance, we found that among child abuse pediatricians, the connection between compassion fatigue and burnout disappears in the presence of hope.

Another example we found is that for parents who must go through programming to be reunified with their children, those with higher hope actually complete programming faster and at a higher rate of success than lower hope parents

So, if we begin to think about doing work with vulnerable populations, it seems to me that we need to do so in the context of nurturing hope.

Q: How can churches and pastors be better equipped to play a role in giving hope to those who are dealing with trauma?

A: Part of the early work we did with hope is demonstrating that hope can be learned. While this may be influenced a little by a personality, we have shown that we can teach hopeful thinking.

A goal of mine for 2020 is to create the framework for a hope-centered organization and a toolkit that people can use to integrate in that context. And while I do a lot of my work in the nonprofit world, I actually think that this work with churches is just such a perfect combination. In all honesty, when I think about hope and grace, I don't see how those are very separate at all.

Q: Do you feel like the Bible itself plays a role in giving hope? Are those with deep faith better able to handle trauma versus those who do not have that sort of faith?

A: I do think that biblical teachings are sort of a guide, and that the Bible is a moral compass for hope. It provides that sense of agency we need to continue on in the present because what we're working toward in salvation drives us forward, especially in the context of our own trauma and adversity.

DR. CHAN HELLMAN is a professor of social work at the University of Oklahoma and Director of The Hope Research Center. He has written over 150 scientific publications, presented at numerous national and international conferences worldwide and co-authored the award-winning book *Hope Rising: How the Science of Hope Can Change Your Life*. Chan's research is focused on hope as a psychological strength helping children and adults overcome trauma and adversity.

I think that somebody who has a deep faith tends to have both internal and external resources, or pathways, that help them deal with stress.

When we're facing adversity or trauma, it's that capacity to lean into one another that I think gives us hope. But I also think that, internally, a deep robust faith in God and Jesus provides us the framework to endure at a different level because we know it *will* get better.

Chapter Two

COPING WITH TRAUMA

Having examined the gravity of trauma and its effects on people inside and outside the church, let's now consider how people hold up in the face of these experiences and how they see progress and positive change. In addition, what behaviors are helping people cope better with trauma?

Most people say they are coping very or fairly well already, with the majority ranking themselves as coping "fairly well." (Respondents rated how well they were coping with trauma on a four-point scale, from "very well" to "not well at all," and they also had the option to decline to answer.)

The biggest factors in how well someone is coping are the severity and recency of the trauma. As might be expected, the less severe, the better someone copes with it; the more distant, the better someone copes with it. These factors have a dramatic effect on coping—but they are not often within a person's control and raise a question of whether time is more effective in bringing about either perspective or solutions.

Religion does seem to affect how well a person copes with trauma. Three in 10 practicing Christians are coping very well. This percentage declines among non-practicing Christians (20%) and non-Christians (14%). Similar percentages—a little more than half—across the three groups reports coping fairly well, but there are divergences at the other extreme; 16 percent of practicing Christians, compared to 25 percent of non-practicing Christians and 28 percent of non-Christians, say they are coping not very well or not well at all.

Using people's personal perceptions of how well they are coping as a metric for healing, researchers looked at how a number of factors in

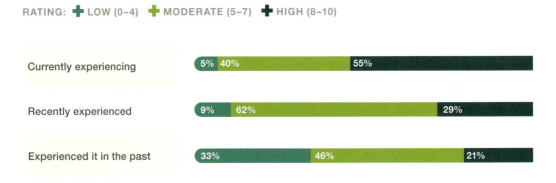

SELF-RATED SEVERITY OF TRAUMA AMONG PRACTICING CHRISTIANS, BY HOW WELL THEY'RE COPING & HOW RECENT THE EVENT WAS

RATING: ✚ LOW (0–4) ✚ MODERATE (5–7) ✚ HIGH (8–10)

	Low	Moderate	High
Currently experiencing	5%	40%	55%
Recently experienced	9%	62%	29%
Experienced it in the past	33%	46%	21%

n=1,015 practicing Christian adults who experienced trauma; June 6–28, 2019.

combination affect progress, paying special attention to the difference Christian practice and church interventions made.

When factors that make a difference—such as income, age, ethnicity, severity and recency of trauma—are taken into account, it turns out that seeking help for trauma from the church does not make a reliable difference in how well a trauma sufferer copes.

However, *Bible use* is linked to how well people cope with their trauma, on its own and when related factors are controlled for. Those who engage with the Bible cope with trauma better than those who do not use the Bible.

The timing of when a person turns to the Bible also affects how well they report coping with trauma. Regardless of the severity of the

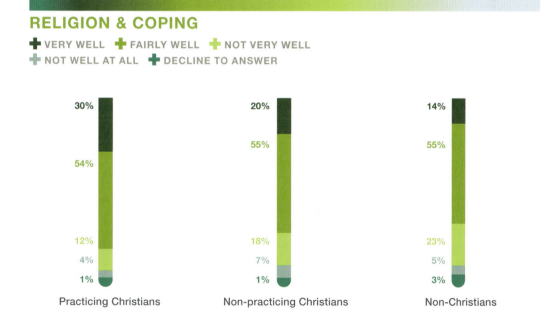

RELIGION & COPING

✚ VERY WELL ✚ FAIRLY WELL ✚ NOT VERY WELL
✚ NOT WELL AT ALL ✚ DECLINE TO ANSWER

Practicing Christians
- 30%
- 54%
- 12%
- 4%
- 1%

Non-practicing Christians
- 20%
- 55%
- 18%
- 7%
- 1%

Non-Christians
- 14%
- 55%
- 23%
- 5%
- 3%

n=2,019 adults who experienced trauma; June 6–28, 2019.

trauma or the person's age, starting to read the Bible specifically because of trauma improves coping levels. Engagement with the Bible prior to experiencing trauma also has some positive impact. On the other hand, people who *stopped* reading the Bible following a trauma report greater difficulty with coping, even more so than those who have never read the Bible at all.

The difference may lie in *how* rather than *whether* people use the Bible to help with their trauma, or perhaps that the benefits of frequent Bible use are correlated with at a certain level of familiarity or fluency with it.

These results also indicate that the value of being a part of the church is not purely social—meaning there are clear benefits from

Bible use is linked to how well people cope with their trauma

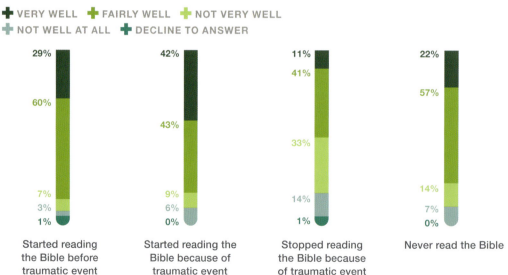

HOW WELL PRACTICING CHRISTIANS ARE COPING AND TIMING OF BIBLE READING

✛ VERY WELL ✛ FAIRLY WELL ✛ NOT VERY WELL
✛ NOT WELL AT ALL ✛ DECLINE TO ANSWER

Started reading the Bible before traumatic event
29%
60%
7%
3%
1%

Started reading the Bible because of traumatic event
42%
43%
9%
6%
0%

Stopped reading the Bible because of traumatic event
11%
41%
33%
14%
1%

Never read the Bible
22%
57%
14%
7%
0%

n=978 practicing Christian adults who experienced trauma; June 6–28, 2019.

interacting with the content of Christianity (not least the Bible), rather than solely the friendships, connections to people who can help or communal activities that happen at church.

WHAT PEOPLE EXPERIENCE AS HELPFUL

The following charts show the proportion of practicing Christians who tried a resource to cope with trauma, then the proportion of the total who consider it one of three most helpful resources, and what proportion of those who chose an option found it to be among the most helpful.

Traumatized practicing Christians are most likely to seek help from God (52%), family members (39%) and friends (37%). For other

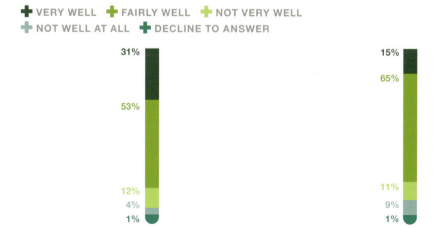

HOW WELL PRACTICING CHRISTIANS ARE COPING & BIBLE USE

✚ VERY WELL ✚ FAIRLY WELL ✚ NOT VERY WELL
✚ NOT WELL AT ALL ✚ DECLINE TO ANSWER

Turned to the Bible for help with trauma
- 31%
- 53%
- 12%
- 4%
- 1%

Did not turn to the Bible for help with trauma
- 15%
- 65%
- 11%
- 9%
- 1%

n=978 practicing Christian adults who experienced trauma; June 6–28, 2019.

SOUGHT HELP FOR TRAUMA FROM…

+ PRACTICING CHRISTIANS   **+** NON-PRACTICING CHRISTIANS   **+** NON-CHRISTIANS

	Practicing Christians	Non-Practicing Christians	Non-Christians
God / the Bible	52%	26%	12%
Family member	39%	33%	37%
Friend	37%	36%	49%
Professional counselor or psychologist / psychiatrist	26%	25%	35%
Self-help books, pamphlets or articles	25%	18%	22%
Someone at a church / parish	25%	8%	3%
Spouse or significant other	24%	22%	30%
Medical professional	18%	17%	23%
An online community	10%	7%	15%
Co-worker	8%	5%	8%
Social worker	7%	7%	11%
Police or another public servant	4%	4%	6%
Someone at a synagogue or mosque	2%	2%	3%
Did not seek help from anyone	9%	17%	13%

n=2,000 adults who experienced trauma; June 6–28, 2019.

resources, they are most likely to say they went to the Bible (55%) or other Christian resources (30%). Seventeen percent did not seek help from non-human resources, and 9 percent did not seek help from any person.

Traumatized non-practicing Christians look first to community, being most likely to seek help from a friend (36%) or family member (33%). For other resources, they are most likely to say they went to the Bible (26%), medical information (22%) or self-help resources (18%). But two in five (39%) did not seek help from non-human resources, and 17 percent did not seek help from any person.

Traumatized non-Christians also lean first on friends (49%) and family members (37%), as well as professional counselors (35%). For other resources, they look to medical information (27%) or self-help resources (22%). Like non-practicing Christians, two in five (40%) did

RESOURCES TURNED TO FOR TRAUMA

+ PRACTICING CHRISTIANS **+** NON-PRACTICING CHRISTIANS **+** NON-CHRISTIANS

The Bible	55%	26%	9%
Other Christian resources	30%	17%	4%
Religious / faith-oriented books (other than Christian)	23%	11%	9%
Medical research / articles	22%	22%	27%
Did not seek help from any resources	17%	39%	40%

n=1,734 U.S. adults who sought some sort of help for trauma; June 6–28, 2019.

not seek help from non-human resources, and 13 percent did not seek help from any person.

Given the relatively high rates of practicing Christians seeking help from people and resources, they seem to have a network of help they can and do use more frequently.

NEGATIVE FEELINGS ASSOCIATED WITH TRAUMA

Most practicing Christians—two-thirds (65% vs. 42% of others)—say they knew God was with them in their trauma. This reassurance does not entirely crowd out other questions, however. For instance, 37 percent of practicing Christians and 43 percent of non-practicing

NEGATIVE RESPONSES TO TRAUMA AMONG PRACTICING CHRISTIANS

Some people who have experienced trauma also struggle with negative feelings which may or may not be true, but are still felt. After experiencing this trauma, to what extent did you feel that …

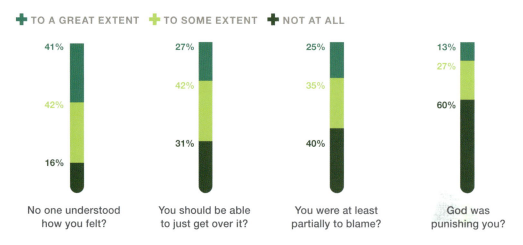

✚ TO A GREAT EXTENT   ✚ TO SOME EXTENT   ✚ NOT AT ALL

	No one understood how you felt?	You should be able to just get over it?	You were at least partially to blame?	God was punishing you?
To a great extent	41%	27%	25%	13%
To some extent	42%	42%	35%	27%
Not at all	16%	31%	40%	60%

n=996 practicing Christians who experienced trauma; June 6–28, 2019.

Christians report asking why God allows suffering. Additionally, one-fifth of practicing Christians (21%) and one-quarter of non-practicing Christians (26%) began to question the goodness of God during their trial.

So how do people explain their trauma? What other negative thoughts or experiences accompany the traumatic event? What signs are there of moral or theological assumptions about the nature of trauma? Researchers asked a series of questions that reveal some of these answers, and both Christians—practicing and non-practicing—gave remarkably similar responses concerning a sense of guilt, shame, isolation or frustration.

Most practicing Christians—two-thirds—say they knew God was with them in their trauma

NEGATIVE RESPONSES TO TRAUMA AMONG NON-PRACTICING CHRISTIANS & NON-CHRISTIANS

Some people who have experienced trauma also struggle with negative feelings which may or may not be true, but are still felt. After experiencing this trauma, to what extent did you feel that …

✚ TO A GREAT EXTENT ✚ TO SOME EXTENT ✚ NOT AT ALL

No one understood how you felt?
- 41%
- 43%
- 16%

You should be able to just get over it?
- 23%
- 48%
- 28%

You were at least partially to blame?
- 23%
- 35%
- 42%

God was punishing you?
- 15%
- 28%
- 57%

n=967 non-practicing Christian and non-Christian adults who experienced trauma; June 6–28, 2019.

Forty-one percent of both practicing Christians and non-practicing Christians / non-Christians affirm that to a great extent it seemed no one else understood how they felt in times of trauma. One in four (27% practicing Christians, 23% others) strongly believes they should just be able to get over their feelings. Another half of non-practicing Christians and non-Christians (48%) and two-fifths of practicing Christians (42%) at least somewhat embrace this idea.

One-third of traumatized respondents feels to some extent they were partially to blame for their suffering, one-quarter (25% practicing Christians, 23% others) strongly so. Two-fifths of non-practicing Christians and non-Christians (42%) and practicing Christians (40%) do not feel this way at all.

Across faith groups, about one-third experiences guilt or shame, with one-fifth doing so often. Two-thirds never encounter these feelings. Though one might assume some religious teachings around sin

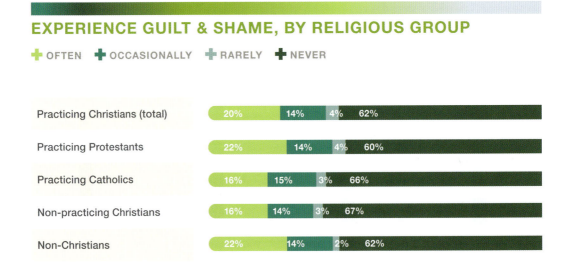

EXPERIENCE GUILT & SHAME, BY RELIGIOUS GROUP

✚ OFTEN ✚ OCCASIONALLY ✚ RARELY ✚ NEVER

Group	Often	Occasionally	Rarely	Never
Practicing Christians (total)	20%	14%	4%	62%
Practicing Protestants	22%	14%	4%	60%
Practicing Catholics	16%	15%	3%	66%
Non-practicing Christians	16%	14%	3%	67%
Non-Christians	22%	14%	2%	62%

n=2,004 adults who experienced trauma; June 6–28, 2019.

and suffering might foster feelings of guilt or shame, church participation or even identifying as a Christian do not seem to make an overall difference. Nor does denomination, although a particular community's teachings may have an effect not visible in this data.

An exception occurs among practicing Christians whose traumatic event involved addiction, 59 percent of whom say they feel guilt or shame. Among non-practicing Christians and non-Christians, this is true for 55 percent of those with addiction experiences.

This study also gives no reason to suppose people who seek help from churches or from Scripture are generally made to feel guilty. Practicing Christians who sought help from a church are actually less likely to feel guilt or shame than those who sought help from a professional counselor (41% vs. 51%) and no more likely to feel guilty than those who sought no help at all.

Practicing Christians who turned to the Bible for help with their trauma are also less likely than those who did not to experience guilt (37% vs. 49%). The same pattern held among non-practicing Christians and non-Christians, with one-third of those who turned to the Bible (32%) and two-fifths of those who did not (40%) experiencing guilt or shame.

This is not to say that there is no variation in frequency of guilt or shame among traumatized people. However, instead of falling into categories by faith group, other demographic and life experiences affect their experience with guilt or shame. Across the board, women are more likely than men (41% vs. 31%), younger adults are more likely than older adults (44% Millennials, 42% Gen X, 27% Boomers) and less-educated adults are more likely than well-educated adults (39% high school vs. 31% college graduates) to experience guilt or shame.

Being a primary victim rather than only a witness of trauma increases the likelihood that an individual encounters guilt or shame (43% vs. 26% among practicing Christians; 40% vs. 19% among others).

Unsurprisingly, people who are coping well feel less guilty or shamed (28% of practicing Christians, 22% of others). Six in 10 practicing Christians (57%) and four in 10 others (42%) who say they are not coping well do encounter these negative emotions. A similar but less dramatic relationship is seen in the influence of severity of trauma; 45 percent of practicing Christians and 40 percent of others with severe trauma feel guilt or shame, while 29 percent of practicing Christians and 24 percent of others with low severity of trauma report this experience. In sum, guilt and shame, when present, are usually tied to demographic characteristics and elements of trauma itself.

Whatever their feelings of guilt, most of the traumatized do not feel God was punishing them (60% practicing Christians vs. 57% non-practicing Christians and non-Christians), though one in seven non-practicing Christians and non-Christians (15%) and practicing Christians (13%) think God was punishing them to a great extent. Practicing Catholics are more likely than practicing Protestants to feel this way (20% vs. 10%). The people most likely to perceive trauma as God's punishment seem to be those who are not close to Scripture and whose trauma is very intense; that is, practicing Christians who are currently experiencing a traumatic event (32%), those with a high degree of trauma (22%) or those who read the Bible less than a few times a year (20%).

Pastors will want to pay attention to the isolation and frustration that most people feel following their traumatic events. They may also want to make sure that congregants understand the theology of suffering—to the extent possible—and how to handle guilt, real or imagined.

> **Guilt and shame, when present, are usually tied to demographic characteristics and elements of trauma itself**

GOD'S NEARNESS TO THOSE WHO ARE SUFFERING

BY HARRIET HILL

We can think of the Bible as a trauma recovery manual. How did Israel survive as a nation? The Bible is full of stories of trauma, suffering and God's deliverance. These stories give us hope that even when we are suffering, God will deliver us. One part of lamenting is remembering God's goodness in the past—whether that is directed at us personally or at his people. From the tree in the Garden whose misuse brought death and all it entails (sickness, suffering, violence and so forth) to the tree in Revelation 22 whose leaves heal the nations, the Bible is full of stories that show God's constant care and power, especially for those who are suffering. He is concerned for justice and is especially close to those who are brokenhearted, to the foreigner and to the oppressed.

At the heart of the biblical narrative is our suffering Savior, who understands what suffering feels like, and whose stripes heal our pain and the pain of the whole world. And his resurrection gives us hope that our suffering will not be eternal. Whether in this life or the next, we will be completely healed, all tears wiped away, and we will be free of death.

NEGATIVE FEELINGS ASSOCIATED WITH TRAUMA

Reading the Bible through the lens of trauma, we see that in times of suffering, God's people lament. Job wrestles verbally with God, pouring out his questions about why God has allowed him to suffer, expressing his anger and depression, and even questioning God's goodness. Lamenting and wrestling with God are signs of faith—that we believe God is there, that he is listening, that he can do something. By expressing our pain and doubt, we clear the way and make room for joy to fill our hearts.

Lament helps us heal from trauma. Silencing our pain and questions under the guise of faith is fatal to a vibrant relationship with God.

HOW CHURCHES CAN HELP

Trauma isolates. Healing requires being in community and in relationship with others. It can be easier to form relationships in a smaller church.

Whether small or large, however, churches need basic skills in responding to trauma and suffering: understanding the effects of trauma, learning to feel our emotions and work with them, learning to lament, learning to listen, learning to bring our pain to Christ and ask for healing as well as learning what forgiveness is and how to forgive from the heart.

It is wonderful to have counselors available at a church. Whether that is possible or not, all church members can acquire basic skills that infuse the church with helpful responses to trauma. These skills are not complex and are a helpful complement where professional counselors are available. In the end, it is not what people do in a counseling session but what they do outside counseling sessions in ordinary life that matters most.

We have found that churches, large and small, that have become competent in trauma healing have grown in their vibrancy, participation, harmony, love of the Bible and ministry to others.

HOW LOVED ONES CAN HELP

One of the first criteria for being able to help family and friends who are experiencing trauma is that you have embraced your own pain—be it small or large—and experienced the healing process. Since the whole creation is affected by the fall, everyone has some pain. If you are harsh on yourself, you will not be able to be empathetic to others. If you are preoccupied with your own unresolved issues, you will not be able to attend to others and listen well.

Acquiring skills for helping others is an experiential process, like riding a bike. It must be done in relationship. You can't just read a manual. Churches and communities can be places where this kind of experience is available.

DR. HARRIET HILL is a pioneer in developing Bible-based trauma healing materials and programs that help church leaders heal from trauma and then help their people heal. Since its start in 2001, the program has spread to around 100 countries with around 15,000 trained facilitators. Harriet holds a Ph.D. from Fuller Seminary in Intercultural Studies. Prior to involvement in trauma healing, she served with Wycliffe and SIL International for 33 years in Bible translation and Scripture engagement. She is on staff at American Bible Society in Philadelphia and has three children and five grandchildren.

Chapter Three

WHAT CHURCHES CAN DO

If someone who has experienced trauma was interested in a church's help, would they be able to find it? It seems likely. For the group in this survey who know churches best—practicing Christians—four out of five are aware of at least one way their churches provide help to those with trauma.

Roughly one-third says their churches offer counseling services, either with a professional counselor (36%) or a non-professional church staff member (32%). A similar proportion (35%) says their churches refer to resources outside the church, which might also include counseling. Other methods of support include preachers giving messages from the pulpit about trauma or suffering (29%) or offering classes or support groups for trauma healing (21%).

Only 7 percent of the respondents say their church provides no specific help for people who have experienced trauma, although an additional 18 percent admit not being aware if such offerings exist. It's possible that some of those whose trauma occurred a long time ago or those who have not sought help at their church may incorrectly believe the church offers nothing for their situation, though some might know from experience that their churches provide little or no help.

A practicing Christian's experience of what a church offers for trauma varies by generation, which may be due to the different types of churches people of different generations attend. For example, more than half of Millennials (54%), compared to less than one-third of Gen X (29%) and Boomers (27%), go to a church that has a professional counselor at the church.

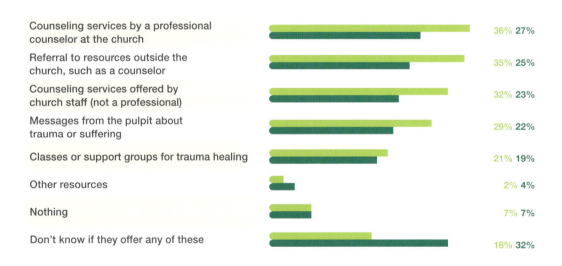

WHAT PEOPLE SAY THEIR CHURCHES OFFER

✚ PRACTICING CHRISTIANS ✚ ALL NON-PRACTICING CHRISTIANS AND NON-CHRISTIANS

	Practicing Christians	All Non-Practicing Christians and Non-Christians
Counseling services by a professional counselor at the church	36%	27%
Referral to resources outside the church, such as a counselor	35%	25%
Counseling services offered by church staff (not a professional)	32%	23%
Messages from the pulpit about trauma or suffering	29%	22%
Classes or support groups for trauma healing	21%	19%
Other resources	2%	4%
Nothing	7%	7%
Don't know if they offer any of these	18%	32%

n=1,138 adults who experienced trauma and attended church at least once in the past month; June 6–28, 2019.

Among both non-practicing Christians and non-Christians, the pattern in reported available resources is similar but lower, with one-third being unsure of what their churches offer (32%).

What do clergy say they do when someone with trauma comes to them for help?

When a person in their congregation is facing a crisis, four in five Protestant pastors (80%) say they typically set up counseling with a pastor at the church and refer the individual to a professional counselor. Three-quarters (76%) offer to pray with the congregant. Seven in 10 Protestant pastors (71%) say they offer some type of counseling service to congregants.

Mainline pastors are more likely to refer someone to a professional counselor outside the church (91% vs. 76% non-mainline), while non-mainline pastors are more likely to offer counseling in the church with a pastor (84% vs. 72% mainline). This is likely related to mainline churches' lower rate of having professionally trained counselors on staff.

More than half of the Protestant pastors in this study (55%) report having someone on staff who has received professional counseling training or mental health training. Forty-three percent of senior Protestant pastors have received this training themselves, though lay leaders (24%) or other church staff members (12%) may have as well. Still, two in five (41%) indicate that no church employee has received professional counseling training or mental health training.

While Catholic priests are less likely than Protestant pastors to set up a counseling session with individuals themselves, they are just as likely to pray with parishioners or refer people to professional counselors. Many Catholic parishes have the added option of referring congregants to a program through the diocese or archdiocese (57%).

The biggest predictor of what churches may or may not be able to provide is church size, which can mean greater capacity, more connections and financial resources. This factor also overlaps somewhat with denomination in this survey; Mainline churches on average (mean) have 138 attendees, while non-mainline churches have an average of 201.

Seven out of 10 Protestant pastors in churches of 250 or more people (70%) say they have a professionally trained person on staff, which is true of a little more than half of smaller churches (58% of churches of fewer than 100 people, 57% of churches of between 100 and 249 people).

The discrepancy between what practicing Christians and pastors say churches offer raises questions. Are practicing Christians underestimating what churches offer for trauma? Are Protestant

The biggest predictor of what churches may or may not be able to provide is church size

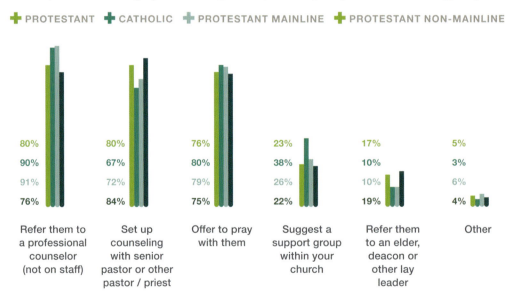

HELP OFFERED BY PASTORS & PRIESTS

When a person in the congregation is facing a crisis, what do you / your staff members typically do?

✚ PROTESTANT   ✚ CATHOLIC   ✚ PROTESTANT MAINLINE   ✚ PROTESTANT NON-MAINLINE

	Refer them to a professional counselor (not on staff)	Set up counseling with senior pastor or other pastor / priest	Offer to pray with them	Suggest a support group within your church	Refer them to an elder, deacon or other lay leader	Other
Protestant	80%	80%	76%	23%	17%	5%
Catholic	90%	67%	80%	38%	10%	3%
Protestant Mainline	91%	72%	79%	26%	10%	6%
Protestant Non-Mainline	76%	84%	75%	22%	19%	4%

n=569 U.S. clergy; June 7–26, 2019.

pastors over-reporting the counseling or referrals that actually happen through their churches? Are practicing Christians disproportionately going to under-resourced churches?

While it may not need to be a weekly messaging point, pastors might consider making sure their congregants know what help is available to them. Of the 53 percent of Protestant pastors who have addressed trauma from the pulpit, 48 percent say this included informing congregants about how the church could help people. Therefore, just one in four Protestant pastors (26%) have explicitly shared from the pulpit in the past six months about how their churches can support people experiencing trauma.

HELP OFFERED BY PROTESTANT PASTORS, BY CHURCH SIZE

When a person in the congregation is facing a crisis, what do you / your staff members typically do?

✚ UNDER 100 PEOPLE ✚ 100–249 PEOPLE ✚ 250+ PEOPLE

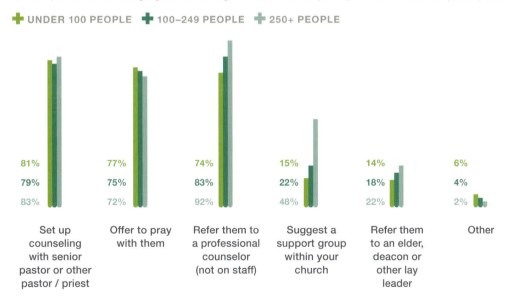

	Set up counseling with senior pastor or other pastor / priest	Offer to pray with them	Refer them to a professional counselor (not on staff)	Suggest a support group within your church	Refer them to an elder, deacon or other lay leader	Other
	81%	77%	74%	15%	14%	6%
	79%	75%	83%	22%	18%	4%
	83%	72%	92%	48%	22%	2%

n=509 U.S. Protestant pastors; June 7–26, 2019.

WHEN PEOPLE GET HELP FROM THE CHURCH

As mentioned in the previous chapter, church leaders and other forms of spiritual help are elements of a range of possible resources that help people through trauma. One-quarter of practicing Christians (25%) indicates "someone at a church / parish" has been a source of help or comfort as they've coped with trauma. Sixty-one percent of those practicing Christians sought out senior pastors and three in 10 (29%) went to another pastor. The recency of the traumatic event does not influence the likelihood of practicing Christians seeking church help.

Other respondents (6%), including non-practicing Christians (8%), are generally much less likely to go to someone at a church for support. Just 3 percent of non-Christians would consider this option.

This indicates that many of those suffering from trauma in churches will not approach church leadership. Even among more committed attendees, three-quarters of those suffering from trauma are engaging with the Church but not regarding it as a source of help. And of those outside the Church, it is a rare thing even for self-identified Christians to navigate trauma with aid from their church.

That doesn't mean, however, that Christians are not seeking spiritual solutions outside their church leadership. Most say they look for help from "God / the Bible" (52%) and use the Bible as a resource (55%). These are options relied upon even more commonly than family members (39%).

And there is still good news for both churches who offer help and people who receive it: Those who seek support from a church to deal with trauma are generally satisfied. More than half of practicing Christians who sought a church's support for their trauma (55%) indicate a high level of satisfaction, while another third (33%) is somewhat satisfied, meaning only a minority (12%) feels assistance from their church was not adequate on some level.

It seems likely that some characteristics of those who seek help from a church affect how well they respond to the Church's help—particularly their greater engagement with the Bible. Those who solicit help from the Church make up a larger-than-average proportion of those who used their Bibles weekly or more (77%) and those who also engaged with the Bible before experiencing a trauma (65%).

There are no signs that seeking spiritual help "crowds out" an individual's engagement with other valuable forms of support. Looking at practicing Christians, there are no resources or individuals a person is less likely to seek out if they have turned to either a church or Scripture for help with their trauma. In fact, using the Bible is usually associated with a greater likelihood of seeking other kinds of help.

Those who seek support from a church to deal with trauma are generally satisfied

PRACTICING CHRISTIANS' SATISFACTION WITH HELP FOR TRAUMA FROM THE CHURCH

✚ VERY SATISFIED   ✚ SOMEWHAT SATISFIED
✚ SOMEWHAT DISSATISFIED   ✚ VERY DISSATISFIED

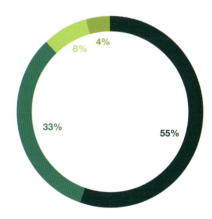

- 55% — Very satisfied
- 33% — Somewhat satisfied
- 8% — Somewhat dissatisfied
- 4% — Very dissatisfied

n=243 practicing Christian adults who sought help from the church for trauma support; June 6–28, 2019.

As only a small number of non-practicing Christians and non-Christians have engaged with help from a church, this picture is less clear among those less engaged with faith, but there is still little indication that seeking church help makes one significantly less likely to look to other resources.

OPENNESS TO THE CHURCH'S HELP WITH TRAUMA

Given that a small proportion of people, Christian or otherwise, seek help from the Church for trauma, what might help more individuals make the connection? This study also gauges respondents' openness

PRACTICING CHRISTIANS SEEKING HELP FROM THE CHURCH, BY RECENCY OF TRAUMA

Imagine that a church in your area offered help to people who had experienced trauma. How likely would you be to seek help from such a church if it was a type of church that you were familiar with?

✚ VERY LIKELY   ✚ SOMEWHAT LIKELY   ✚ SOMEWHAT UNLIKELY   ✚ VERY UNLIKELY

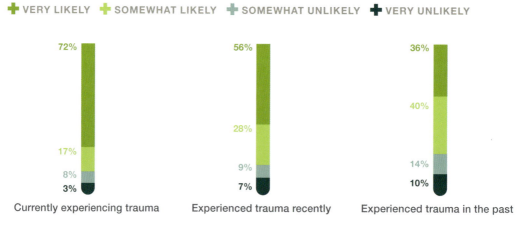

Currently experiencing trauma: 72% / 17% / 8% / 3%
Experienced trauma recently: 56% / 28% / 9% / 7%
Experienced trauma in the past: 36% / 40% / 14% / 10%

n=755 practicing Christian adults who experienced trauma and did not seek help from a church; June 6–28, 2019.

to help from churches and suggests that even people with limited relationships to faith are at least open to a church's help.

People who have not already sought help from a church (74% of practicing Christians and 92% of others) answered the question, "Imagine that a church in your area offered help to people who had experienced trauma. How likely would you be to seek help from such a church if it were a type of church that you were familiar with?" The average response from practicing Christians is that they are "somewhat likely" to seek help for trauma in church. Most practicing Christians (79%) say they would be likely to seek help from a church that offered help with trauma. So does a slight majority of non-practicing Christians (56%). A minority of these groups (9% practicing, 24% non-practicing) is closed to the idea of receiving support from

Even people with limited relationships to faith are at least open to a church's help

SEEKING HELP FROM THE CHURCH

Imagine that a church in your area offered help to people who had experienced trauma. How likely would you be to seek help from such a church if it was a type of church that you were familiar with?

✛ VERY LIKELY ✛ SOMEWHAT LIKELY ✛ SOMEWHAT UNLIKELY ✛ VERY UNLIKELY

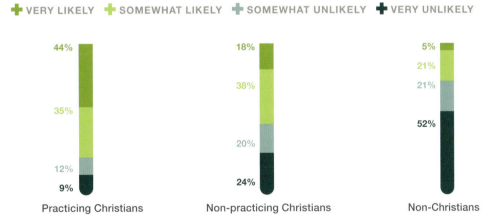

Practicing Christians
44%
35%
12%
9%

Non-practicing Christians
18%
38%
20%
24%

Non-Christians
5%
21%
21%
52%

n=1,665 adults who experienced trauma and did not seek help from a church; June 6–28, 2019.

HELPING THE CHURCH BECOME A RESOURCE
BY HEATHER DREW

Church hurt is real. It only takes one painful church experience for someone to be afraid it could happen again. If a traumatized person seeks help in a church community and does not receive safety, understanding, acknowledgement, patience and compassion (among other things), they may become more hurt, and this second wound can be more painful than the first. If a survivor has experienced church hurt, trust must be earned over time. Expecting a person who has been hurt to trust quickly is the first mistake to be corrected. When church communities have information about what normal responses to trauma are, it may make it easier for them to provide safety and belonging and to become the refuges for survivors.

When people have experienced a traumatic event, their primary need is safety and stabilization. Once their basic physiological needs are met, they are out of immediate danger and have personal security (employment, access to resources, health, etc.), they can continue to function, even though this happens at a different level than before the incident. This also means that they need to experience emotional safety within their communities—that friends, family and church leaders do not demand immediate healing.

HEATHER DREW, MA, LPC works as a writer, speaker, teacher and licensed professional counselor and is currently on staff at American Bible Society as a trauma healing training manager. She holds a Master of Arts in Professional Counseling and a post-graduate certificate in Global Trauma Recovery. For 17 years she has worked with people who live with stories of trauma and abuse, helping individuals from a vast array of cultural, socioeconomic and spiritual backgrounds.

The second thing a person in trauma recovery needs is a safe space to process their emotions and painful experiences. This is the stage of recovery when a person may relive and / or remember traumatic experiences and require people whom they can talk to about the event. They need space to share and process what happened, how they feel and what is / was hardest for them. Most of all, they need to know that whatever they share will not cause them to be judged or condemned by the listener. This stage of healing requires patience, compassion and empathic listening from the helper. If church communities can provide these things, they may be more readily considered resources and refuges for survivors.

a church. Meanwhile, over half of non-Christians (52%) say they are very unlikely to consider the Church as a source of trauma help, though one-quarter (26%) is at least somewhat open to the idea.

This is not an insignificant level of openness, particularly among those with frequent engagement with the Church. What might keep this group from actually seeking help for trauma in a church context? For one thing, most feel that their traumatic event is behind them; practicing Christians who are currently experiencing trauma (72%) are more likely than those who recently (56%) or previously (36%) experienced trauma to say they are open to help from a church. Using regression analysis to evaluate several factors at once (the severity of trauma, the recency of a traumatic event, age, how well someone is

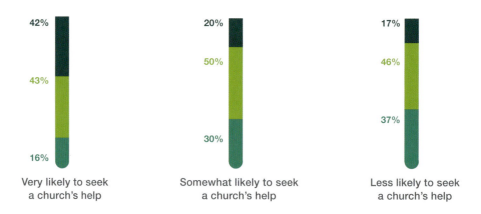

SEVERITY OF TRAUMA AMONG PRACTICING CHRISTIANS WHO HAVEN'T YET SOUGHT HELP FROM A CHURCH

✚ HIGH (8–10) ✚ MODERATE (5–7) ✚ LOW (0–4)

Very likely to seek a church's help
- 42%
- 43%
- 16%

Somewhat likely to seek a church's help
- 20%
- 50%
- 30%

Less likely to seek a church's help
- 17%
- 46%
- 37%

n=755 practicing Christian adults who experienced trauma but did not seek out help from a church; June 6–28, 2019.

coping, how well a person rates the Church's ability to help and whether a person is a practicing Christian), researchers determined that severity and recency of trauma indeed have the most significant effect on an individual's willingness to seek church help. The more severe people rate their trauma, the more likely they are to say they're open to help from the Church. A person's trust in the Church's ability to help and whether they are already practicing Christians also have some bearing.

In Barna Group's *The Connected Generation* study, Barna learned that American Millennial "nomads," who identify as Christian but are not attending a church, agree that people at church are judgmental (55%) and that the Church does not (27%) or cannot (23%) answer their questions. They also agree that people at church are "too good" and "too holy" for them (20%). While we cannot say these young adults have been hurt by the Church, we can say that in comparison to attending Christians, nomads are less likely to see the Church as a place to take their struggles.

WHAT PEOPLE WANT FROM CHURCH PROGRAMS

People who either had turned to a church for help or who are open to turning to a church for help with their trauma answered a series of questions about what they hope a church could offer.

For practicing Christians, the most important aspects of a trauma program in a church are connecting with God and learning how to experience his comfort (79%) and finding a way to heal your heart (78%). Non-practicing Christians and non-Christians consider feeling less anxiety (68%) as most important (on par with the two-thirds of practicing Christians who hope for this outcome) and are highly motivated by finding a way to heal their hearts (65%).

RESOURCES FOR THE UNEMPLOYED

Among practicing Christians, the unemployed—who more often indicate they are the primary victim of a traumatic event (79% vs. 70% employed)—are less likely than those who are employed full-time to say they are coping very well with their trauma (39% vs. 48%). They also seem to be detached from spiritual solutions.

Unemployed practicing Christians are less likely to turn to the church for help (23%) than those who are employed (30%) and less likely to be open to help from a church (34% vs. 52%). Further, three in five practicing Christians who say they do not know about the church's ability to help with trauma (61%) are unemployed.

It's worth noting that unemployed practicing Christians, as people of faith, are still highly likely to seek help from the Bible (87%) and to be satisfied with a church's help when they seek it (62%)—but all at a lower rate than employed practicing Christians.

Together, these characteristics of unemployed practicing Christians with trauma point to some reluctance to seek help or information on trauma from Christian sources.

This isn't a factor among non-practicing Christians and non-Christians (16% say they are not coping well), however, unemployed non-practicing Christians and non-Christians are more likely to seek no help (18%) or the help of a professional (33%) than to seek a church's help (6%) in addressing trauma.

DIFFERENCES BETWEEN EMPLOYED & UNEMPLOYED SURVIVORS

✚ EMPLOYED PRACTICING CHRISTIANS   ✚ UNEMPLOYED PRACTICING CHRISTIANS
✚ EMPLOYED NON-PRACTICING CHRISTIANS / NON-CHRISTIANS
✚ UNEMPLOYED NON-PRACTICING CHRISTIANS / NON-CHRISTIANS

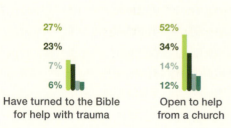

Have turned to the Bible for help with trauma: 27% / 23% / 7% / 6%

Open to help from a church: 52% / 34% / 14% / 12%

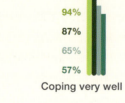

Coping very well: 94% / 87% / 65% / 57%

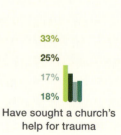

Have sought a church's help for trauma: 33% / 25% / 17% / 18%

n=2,019 adults who experienced trauma; June 6–28, 2019.

PRACTICING CHRISTIANS WHO ARE OPEN TO THE CHURCH'S HELP

If you were considering seeking help from a church to cope with trauma, how important would it be for you to be able to …

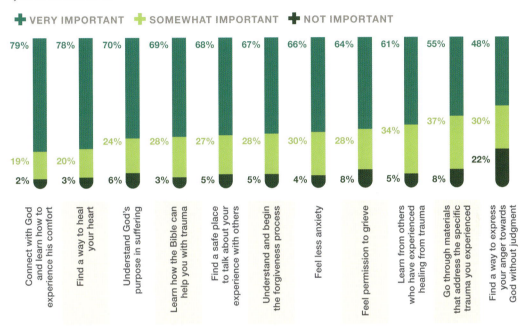

n=817 practicing Christian adults who have turned to the church or who are open to help from the church; June 6–28, 2019.

Practicing Christians also put more emphasis than other respondents on learning how the Bible can help and understanding God's purposes in suffering. And though it's at the bottom of the list, finding a way to express anger toward God is of greater priority to practicing Christians (48% vs. 36%).

Practicing Christian women rank nearly all of these aspects as more important than do their male counterparts. A similar pattern can also be seen among non-practicing Christian and non-Christian women.

NON-PRACTICING CHRISTIANS & NON-CHRISTIANS WHO ARE OPEN TO THE CHURCH'S HELP

If you were considering seeking help from a church to cope with trauma, how important would it be for you to be able to …

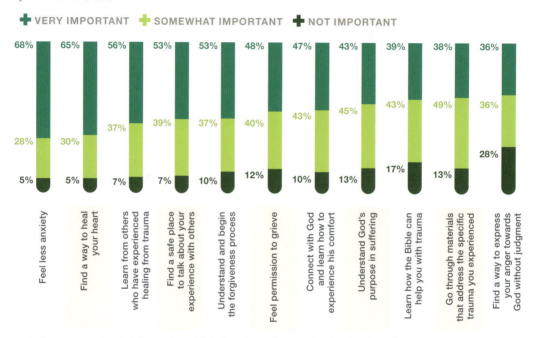

n=436 non-practicing Christian and non-Christian adults who turned to the church or who are open to help from the church; June 6–28, 2019.

 Chapter Four

DEEPENING FAITH DURING TRAUMA

In addition to how well people are coping with their trauma, another important outcome for church leaders to understand is how relationships with God are developed through difficult seasons.

Two-thirds of practicing Christians (65%) say their trauma brought them closer to God. One-third of non-practicing Christians and non-Christians agree. Very few people say it made them lose faith in God (6% non-practicing Christians and non-Christians, 2% practicing Christians). More than one-quarter of non-practicing Christians (28%), however, are in a period of questioning their faith.

People who say they are coping very well with their trauma also tend to say their experience has strengthened their faith. Those who

More than one-quarter of traumatized non-practicing Christians are in a period of questioning their faith

are not faring well are twice as likely as those who are coping fairly well, and six times as likely as those who are coping very well, to say they have questioned their faith.

PRACTICING & NON-PRACTICING CHRISTIANS' FAITH IN GOD AS A RESULT OF TRAUMA

Which of the following best describes what ultimately happened to your faith in God as a result of the trauma you experienced?

n=1,558 adults who experienced trauma; June 6–28, 2019.

COPING & FAITH AMONG PRACTICING CHRISTIANS

Which of the following best describes what ultimately happened to your faith in God as a result of the trauma you experienced?

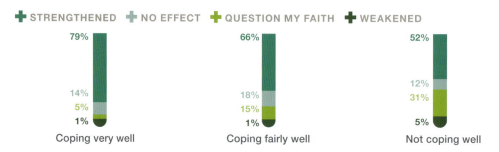

n=994 practicing Christian adults who experienced trauma; June 6–28, 2019.

What leads Christians to find their faith strengthened through trauma? Considering multiple factors at once using regression analysis, researchers found that whether Christians' faith was strengthened could be partially accounted for by a combination of their age, the severity of their trauma, the recency of their trauma and whether they sought help from a church. A separate analysis considered the timing of Christians' Bible use. The results showed that Christians' faith was strengthened if they sought help from someone at a church and if they read the Bible before or because of their trauma. While we do not know if the rate at which people read the Bible changed because of their trauma, we can see that those with a higher frequency of Bible use in general now say their faith was strengthened.

TRAUMATIZED PRACTICING CHRISTIANS' FREQUENCY OF BIBLE USE, BY EFFECT OF TRAUMA ON FAITH

✚ EVERY DAY ✚ FOUR OR MORE TIMES A WEEK ✚ SEVERAL TIMES A WEEK
✚ ONCE A WEEK ✚ ONCE A MONTH ✚ THREE OR FOUR TIMES A YEAR
✚ LESS THAN ONCE A YEAR ✚ NEVER

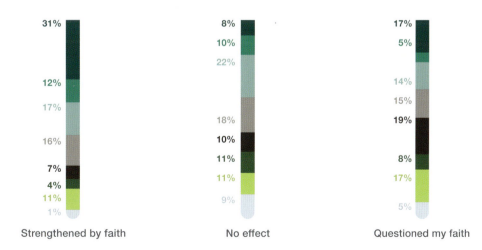

Strengthened by faith: 31%, 12%, 17%, 16%, 7%, 4%, 11%, 1%

No effect: 8%, 10%, 22%, 18%, 10%, 11%, 11%, 9%

Questioned my faith: 17%, 5%, 14%, 15%, 19%, 8%, 17%, 5%

n=988 practicing Christian adults who experienced trauma; June 6–28, 2019.

There is a significant difference in whether Christians say their faith was strengthened according to their timing of going to the Bible. A big difference can be seen in those who were already reading the Bible before they experienced the traumatic event; 57 percent of those whose faith was strengthened were already engaging with Scripture, compared to 48 percent of those whose faith didn't change and 39 percent of those who are questioning their faith. Others turned to the Bible because of their trauma, including a higher proportion of those whose faith is now stronger (19% vs. 11% of those who had no faith change and 9% of those who questioned their faith). Stopping the practice of reading the Bible because of trauma or never reading the Bible at all are, not surprisingly, significantly less likely to strengthen someone's faith.

PRACTICING CHRISTIANS & BIBLE USE

As a result of using the Bible, I ...

✚ VERY STRONGLY AGREE ✚ STRONGLY AGREE ✚ AGREE
✚ SOMEWHAT AGREE ✚ SOMEWHAT DISAGREE ✚ DISAGREE

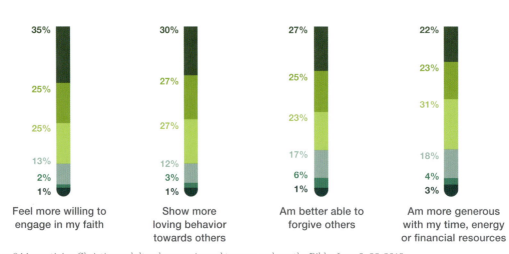

Feel more willing to engage in my faith
35% / 25% / 25% / 13% / 2% / 1%

Show more loving behavior towards others
30% / 27% / 27% / 12% / 3% / 1%

Am better able to forgive others
27% / 25% / 23% / 17% / 6% / 1%

Am more generous with my time, energy or financial resources
22% / 23% / 31% / 18% / 4% / 3%

n=844 practicing Christians adults who experienced trauma and use the Bible; June 6–28, 2019.

NON-PRACTICING CHRISTIANS & BIBLE USE

As a result of using the Bible, I ...

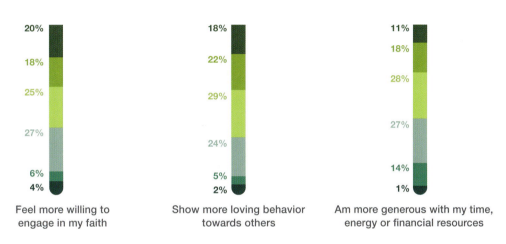

n=275 non-practicing, self-identified Christians who experienced trauma and use the Bible; June 6–28, 2019.

IMPACTS OF ENGAGING SCRIPTURE

What is it about Scripture that might influence or improve a person's faith during a season of trauma? Researchers asked a series of questions among traumatized people who had read the Bible at least once in the past year to gauge possible changes related to Bible engagement.

A third of practicing Christians (35%) and one-fifth of non-practicing Christians (20%) strongly agree that they have become more willing to engage in their faith because of their experience with the Bible. Similar proportions (30% practicing Christians, 18% non-practicing Christians) say that because of their use of the Bible they are more loving toward others. Smaller proportions in both groups (22%

THE ROLE OF FORGIVENESS IN HEALING
BY BRIANNA M. LEIENDECKER

Forgiveness is a process that recognizes someone has sinned against us, accepts the pain this has caused and repeatedly brings that pain to Christ. Jesus taught that forgiveness is an act of obedience to God. It is the choice to let go of the wrongs done against us (see Matthew 6:14–15; Mark 11:25; Luke 17:3–4).

As a spiritual process that is guided by the Holy Spirit, forgiveness involves personal effort and patience. The commitment to forgive often comes before experiencing any feelings of forgiveness. Oftentimes this process can seem to be circular. We begin to forgive a hurt but then circle back to the remembrance of the pain it brought. This repetition is normal. This is a place where Jesus meets us as he invites us to continuously bring that pain and lay it before him. As we repeatedly bring our pain to Jesus, we are moving closer to complete forgiveness and will eventually feel less pain.

Ideas about forgiveness from our culture or tradition can disrupt the healing process of forgiveness. Sometimes people are afraid to forgive because of the misperception that forgiving means minimizing the pain or accepting the offense as normal. Sometimes people believe that forgiveness and reconciliation are the same or occur at the same time. They then expect that trust must immediately be rebuilt between the offender and the victim.

But forgiveness of an offender does not deny the seriousness of the offense, and reconciliation is not a requirement in the healing journey. Reconciliation *may* occur after forgiveness, but if the offender has not repented or changed, reconciliation is neither necessary nor safe.

Forgiveness is instead about releasing our pain and bitterness and letting go of our natural desire for revenge. To remain angry or bitter allows Satan and the traumatic event a foothold into our hearts (Ephesians 4:26–27). If we hold on to anger and bitterness, these feelings will destroy us and affect all aspects of our well-being. They become a form of bondage that will prolong our suffering and will come out in physical and emotional ailments, negative behaviors and increasing isolation from other people. The act of forgiveness frees us and opens us to healing.

It is often difficult to forgive, but Christians are required to do so. The Christian faith is based upon the forgiveness that God extends through his Son. We live in a world damaged by sin and full of offenses and injustices—and none of us is innocent. In his abundant love, God offers us forgiveness by the death and resurrection of

Jesus. When we choose to forgive others, we demonstrate that we understand God's forgiveness and pass on God's love for us.

In the prayer he taught his followers, Jesus has us ask God, "Forgive us the wrongs we have done, as we forgive the wrongs that others have done to us" (Matthew 6:12). He concludes that teaching with a strong statement about his priorities for us and for others: "if you do not forgive others, then your Father will not forgive the wrongs you have done." Jesus came into the world as the great Peacemaker, not only to reconcile humans to God, but to reconcile us to one another.

BRIANNA M. LEIENDECKER, MA serves as the U.S. Trauma Healing Coordinator for American Bible Society. In this responsibility Brianna coordinates the implementation of trauma healing programs in communities and churches throughout the United States. Through the Trauma Healing Institute, she is a certified master facilitator in the small group curriculum, *Healing the Wounds of Trauma: How the Church Can Help*, and travels the country training and certifying others in this curriculum as well. She is a graduate of Biblical Theological Seminary and holds a master's degree in counseling, with which she has provided counseling services to survivors of human trafficking and children who experienced abuse. She currently resides in Delaware with her husband, David.

practicing Christians, 11% non-practicing Christians) say they are more generous because of using the Bible.

Traumatic events, even severe ones, do not necessarily stymie spiritual growth. Still, they are most likely to result in growth for those who are coping well with their trauma. The changes practicing Christians see in themselves are strongest for those who are coping well and who had a high severity of trauma. Forty-five percent of those coping very well and 44 percent of those with a high severity of trauma very strongly agree that they are more willing to engage in their faith. Thirty-one percent of those coping very well and 28 percent with a high severity of trauma very strongly agree that engaging with the Bible has made them more generous. Forty-five percent of those coping very well and 38 percent of those with a high severity of trauma very strongly agree that they have shown more loving behavior toward others as a result of using the Bible.

FINDING FORGIVENESS

Three-quarters of traumatized practicing Christians say that reading the Bible helped them forgive (75%), though they are less likely to agree when they are not coping well. When trauma is more severe, when a practicing Christian uses the Bible more frequently and when they have been engaging with Scripture prior to a traumatic event, a motivation toward forgiveness is more common.

Using regression analysis to consider multiple factors at once, researchers could partially account for the differences in how much the Bible helped traumatized people forgive others, looking at this factor in combination with the severity of their trauma, how well they are coping, how old they are, whether they are practicing Christians and their Bible usage. The results showed that people agree more strongly that the Bible helped them forgive when they are practicing Christians who are coping well and had a previously established habit of reading

Three-quarters of traumatized practicing Christians say that reading the Bible helped them forgive

the Bible. The more severe their trauma and the more they use the Bible, the more likely they are to say Scripture inspired them toward forgiveness.

TRAUMATIZED PRACTICING CHRISTIANS & BIBLE USE

As a result of using the Bible, I am better able to forgive others.

✚ VERY STRONGLY AGREE ✚ STRONGLY AGREE ✚ AGREE
✚ SOMEWHAT AGREE ✚ SOMEWHAT DISAGREE ✚ DISAGREE

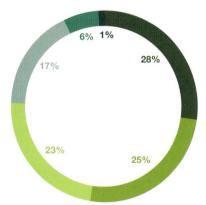

n=844 practicing Christians who experienced trauma and have read the Bible in the past year; June 6–28, 2019.

SAFE RELATIONSHIPS: RESPONSIBLY WALKING ALONGSIDE VICTIMS OF TRAUMA

A Q&A WITH DIANE LANGBERG

Q: Has much changed over the years in regard to what inflicts trauma?

A: Well, to actually call something trauma means that somebody has post-traumatic stress disorder, which is a clinical term that's probably being used more loosely today. Primarily, we see causes such as sexual abuse, rape, domestic violence, war or physical assault that isn't sexual. These things are not statistically extraordinary, but they are overwhelming and can cause natural coping mechanisms to not work.

People who live in unsafe neighborhoods and don't have resources are often traumatized. Most often, trauma has to do with people not being safe and experiencing things that normal coping mechanisms do not work for.

Q: What are some of the issues that people typically face or struggle with as a result of experiencing trauma?

A: Many people try to push it out of their minds and not deal with it, so it continues to be harmful to them. That happens quite often with childhood trauma, as many people don't actually get help for this until they're an adult.

Trauma affects every aspect of being human. It affects the way you think about yourself. In cases of rape or child abuse, for example, a person generally thinks, somehow, that what happened to them was their fault. There are often many physiological symptoms.

Not only is the world unsafe, relationships in particular aren't safe, so people develop "skills" for dealing with relationships where they either become very compliant or very vigilant.

Trauma also affects people spiritually in profound ways. A lot of lies, about the person, about relationships, about God, become present and those lies govern their life.

Q: Have there been any recent developments in your field that have shed a greater light on how to help people cope with and heal from trauma?

A: I'm sure there are new things being introduced all the time, but the bottom line is that the most effective way to help somebody is to work with them in the context of a safe relationship, to help them have a voice, to speak the truth about what happened to them, to wrestle with the lies and to be in a safe relationship with them that treats them completely opposite of how the trauma did.

It takes a very courageous soul to seek help, because, again, they're acknowledging the trauma that they most want to forget and often they're quite sure that people will react in a negative way to that acknowledgement. Anybody who comes forward, whether it's in a clinical relationship, in a church or wherever, is showing tremendous courage. That courage needs to be honored.

Q: How would you assess the ability of pastors to be able to address trauma? How can they become better aware and better equipped?

A: There's certainly no consistent training for this in seminary. Seminary's largely theological in nature, but when you become a pastor, you become a shepherd to many, some of whom have or will experience trauma.

It's not that the church should not be active in helping people deal with trauma. I absolutely think that they can have a tremendous, positive impact, but they have to know what they're doing or they're going to hurt people. They need the humility to say they don't know everything and to ask for help.

A great encouragement to me after all these years is seeing some pastors approach this well

DR. DIANE LANGBERG is a practicing psychologist whose clinical expertise includes 45 years of working with trauma survivors and clergy. She speaks internationally on topics related to trauma, ministry and the Christian life, is the director of Diane Langberg, Ph.D. & Associates and is clinical faculty at Biblical Theological Seminary where she leads the Global Trauma Recovery Institute with Dr. Phil Monroe. A published author, Dr. Langberg is also a columnist for *Christian Counseling Today* and contributes to many other publications.

by sitting through trainings, reading books and seeking consultations when they get stuck.

Helping people cope with and heal from trauma can also be a lay ministry. The pastor doesn't have to do all this alone, though I think they should keep a hand in the process.

Q: Do you think that a Christian's relationship with God changes when they go through trauma?

A: Abuse of any kind is also spiritual abuse. You can't abuse somebody and not do damage spiritually, so you're damaging a person, the way they think about themselves and the way they think about God. For example, the Scriptures say God is our refuge. Really? When someone grows up being abused by their father for 15 years, they may ask, "How is God my refuge?"

They don't even know what refuge means, and so it really does damage to understanding who God is and the truth about him. Everything is filtered through the lens of abuse. That's why providing a safe relationship is the first thing that must be done to help people deal with trauma.

In my experience, living out godly characteristics in front of victims helps them see God in the flesh. Ultimately, what helps them see the reality of God is the cross.

Chapter Five

PASTORS' PREPARATION FOR TRAUMA

In the course of six months, the average (median) pastor sees about two people coming to his or her church seeking help to cope with a traumatic experience. About one-fifth of Protestant pastors (21%) see no one at all seeking help for trauma from their church.

Protestant pastors who say their church has a high demand for counseling receive about 20 people (mean) in a half-year, while those with moderate demand receive about six. The majority of Protestant pastors (69%) says they have low demand and sees about one person each six months approaching the church for help with trauma.

PROTESTANT PASTORS ON THE FREQUENCY OF THE CHURCH BEING USED AS A RESOURCE FOR SURVIVORS

About how many people, if any, have come to your church or parish in the past six months seeking help to cope with or recover from a traumatic experience?

✚ MEAN   ✚ MEDIAN

	Mean	Median
All pastors	5	2
Preached on trauma	7.2	4
Did not preach on trauma	2.5	1
Very well-equipped for trauma	9.6	5
Somewhat equipped for trauma	4.4	2
Not well-equipped for trauma	3.2	2
Church offers counseling	5.7	3
Church doesn't offer counseling	3.3	1
High demand for counseling	19.9	12
Medium demand for counseling	5.6	5
Low demand for counseling	1.5	1
Pastor primary victim of trauma	6.8	3
Pastor witnessed trauma	6.4	3
Pastor neither experienced nor witnessed trauma	3.1	2
250 or more attendees	13	6
100–250 attendees	4	2
Fewer than 100 attendees	2.9	2

n=509 U.S. Protestant pastors; June 7–26, 2019.

While five is the average (mean) number of people seeking help across all Protestant congregations, in churches of 250 or more people it climbs to 13 people, with a median of six. Clearly, larger churches receive a greater number—if not proportion—of people with trauma.

Counseling demand in churches rises along with the church's preparation for trauma. Churches that offer counseling services naturally receive more people who are looking for help, an average (mean) of six.

Counseling demand in churches rises along with the church's preparation for trauma

Interestingly, Protestant pastors who have been neither the primary victim nor a witness of a traumatic event report that fewer congregants come to them for help with trauma. For them, the mean number of people who approached for help with trauma was three, while Protestant pastors who have been more personally affected by trauma saw on average (mean) twice as many (seven for those who were primary victims, and six for those who witnessed a traumatic event). It is possible that Protestant pastors with some experience of trauma seem more approachable to people who are dealing with it.

Perhaps this finding is related to the frequency with which Protestant pastors who have personal experience with trauma speak about trauma from the pulpit—about twice every six months, rather than once. Overall, Protestant pastors who preach on trauma see an average (mean) number of seven people approach their church for help, while Protestant pastors who don't mention trauma see an average (mean) of two. The difference in medians is even more striking: Four for Protestant pastors who preach on trauma, and one for those who don't.

There are several possible reasons for these differences. There may be congregants with trauma who are not approaching the church for help (as, indeed, most don't) but who will come forward when they hear the church is willing and able to help. It may also be that pastors and churches that tell congregants they are willing and able to help with trauma attract traumatized people into the congregation. This may be especially true when a pastor shares a similar background and vulnerabilities as the congregation.

PASTORS' SENSE OF BEING EQUIPPED FOR TRAUMA CARE

Pastors were asked, "How well-equipped do you personally feel to help someone in your congregation deal with significant trauma?" Three-quarters of Protestant pastors (73%) put themselves in the middle as "somewhat equipped." One in seven (15%) feels very well-equipped, while 12 percent do not feel equipped.

When a pastor considers their church well-equipped to handle trauma, there is an average (mean) of 10 people every six months coming in for help with trauma. Those that are somewhat equipped receive four, and those that are not well-equipped receive three. This suggests that about every other month, a church that is not prepared to handle

DO PASTORS FEEL EQUIPPED TO HELP WITH TRAUMA CARE?

VERY WELL-EQUIPPED   SOMEWHAT EQUIPPED   NOT EQUIPPED

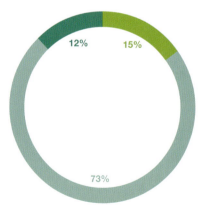

n=569 U.S. Protestant pastors; June 7-26, 2019.

trauma will nevertheless be called on to do so—and if those seeking help stay at that church, their needs accumulate. Trauma is not generally resolved in a matter of weeks or months; those who need help for trauma during one six-month period are likely to still need it the next, and the number of needs may compound—unless the people leave the church or reach a new point in the healing process.

Using regression analysis, researchers examined what elements would make a pastor or priest say they were better prepared. Responses are partially explained by how long the pastor has been in ministry, the size of their church, their type of training for trauma, how many times they have preached about trauma in the past six months and whether or not they have experienced or witnessed any traumatic events.

When all these factors are taken into account, pastors see the biggest boost in feeling prepared to handle trauma when they have preached on it in the past six months, when they have received a master's degree program in therapy or counseling and when they have experienced or witnessed a traumatic event themselves. When pastors have received no training for trauma, they are much less likely to feel prepared.

This finding indicates that a good deal of pastors' preparation to handle trauma in their congregations comes from accumulated experience and training. It also seems to indicate that pastors who have not thought much about trauma, whether via experience, or being trained or teaching their congregations, may be at a disadvantage when a person with trauma comes to their church.

About every other month, a church that is not prepared to handle trauma will nevertheless be called on to do so

PASTORS' TRAINING

The vast majority of Protestant pastors (90%) has received training in counseling. However, this is not always under the direction of a program. Sixty-two percent of Protestant pastors did counseling coursework as part of another degree, while 7 percent have a master's degree in the subject. Some (13%) have done supervised clinical work, while just 1 percent have a therapist licensure or counselor's license. Half (51%) says they have received on-the-job training, though this does not mean that they have not received other training. While Protestant pastors experience greater confidence with most kinds of training, on-the-job training on its own does not produce a significant difference in whether pastors feel well, somewhat or unprepared.

Protestant pastors without training make up a much larger proportion of those who feel unprepared (29%) than of those who feel somewhat (8%) or well-prepared (4%).

Most Protestant pastors (55%) received their training more than 10 years ago, though recency of training does not necessarily produce a positive effect in the way personal experience as a minister does when it comes to a sense of preparation.

PASTORS ON TRAINING TO AID IN RECOVERY AFTER TRAUMA

What type of training, if any, have you received in counseling?

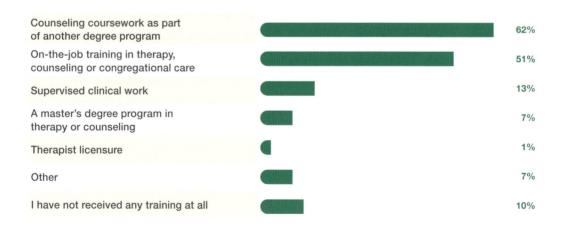

Training type	%
Counseling coursework as part of another degree program	62%
On-the-job training in therapy, counseling or congregational care	51%
Supervised clinical work	13%
A master's degree program in therapy or counseling	7%
Therapist licensure	1%
Other	7%
I have not received any training at all	10%

n=509 U.S. Protestant pastors; June 7–26, 2019.

Despite the boost many pastors get from their training in counseling, when asked, "How well do you think your education or training prepared you to minister to people who have experienced a traumatic event?" most choose "somewhat well" (55%). Just 10 percent choose "very well." About one-third thinks their training did not leave them better equipped (34% "not too well" or "not well at all").

Nearly all Protestant pastors (94% total; 65% somewhat, 29% very much) understand that members of their congregation look to them for help in navigating a trauma. While few in any congregation actually turn to them, that minority of traumatized people may rely on them heavily.

PASTORS' LEVEL OF ISSUE-SPECIFIC PREPARATION

Pastors were asked to select traumatic issues for which they felt well-equipped to provide care, as well as those which they felt poorly equipped to handle. There is a great deal of variation in what pastors feel specifically prepared for.

Most Protestant pastors feel equipped to help during grief over a loved one's death (88%)—the most common form of trauma—as well as divorce (71%), job loss (65%), a serious medical condition (61%), betrayal (57%), destitution (55%) and major financial setbacks (50%).

More than half of Protestant pastors feel unprepared for homicide (54%) and large-scale conflicts (53%).

For most traumatic events, at least a quarter of the group feels neither prepared nor unprepared. Fewer fall into this category when it comes to more common events like the death of a loved one (9%) and divorce (21%). The traumatic events where Protestant pastors are most in-between are trauma through jobs (51%) and burglary or robbery (52%).

However, these are not particularly rare events. First responders, such as EMTs and nurses, physicians, members of the military and

PASTORS' PREPARATION FOR CONGREGANTS FACING TRAUMATIC EVENTS

✚ PREPARED   ✚ NEITHER PREPARED NOR UNPREPARED   ✚ UNPREPARED

Traumatic Event	Prepared	Neither	Unprepared
Death of a loved one	88%	9%	3%
Divorce	71%	21%	8%
Job loss	65%	26%	9%
Diagnosed with a serious medical condition	61%	28%	11%
Betrayal by someone you trusted	57%	32%	11%
Not having enough food, clothing or shelter	55%	33%	12%
Major financial setback	50%	35%	15%
Addiction	45%	27%	28%
Natural disasters	42%	38%	20%
Near death experience or signficant injury	34%	43%	23%
Domestic violence	34%	38%	28%
Suicide	34%	34%	32%
Infertility	33%	35%	32%
Watching someone die or being abused	32%	42%	26%
Prision / incarceration	30%	36%	34%
Sexual abuse	25%	29%	46%
Physical abuse	24%	45%	31%
Burglary / robbery	23%	52%	25%
Racial discrimination	22%	43%	35%
Child abuse	21%	34%	45%
Repeatedly exposed to details about trauma through a job	17%	51%	32%
Large-scale conflicts	12%	35%	53%
Homicide	12%	34%	54%

n=509 U.S. Protestant pastors; June 7–26, 2019.

even clean-up crews and teachers can be exposed to sources of trauma repeatedly through their work. In addition, while few people in this study listed burglary or robbery as a traumatic event, it is not entirely uncommon, with the FBI reporting a rate of property crime of 2,362.2 offenses per 100,000 inhabitants, or about 2 percent.[8]

Note also that more Protestant pastors feel more unprepared than prepared for forms of abuse, such as sexual abuse (46% unprepared), physical abuse (31%) and child abuse (45%), and many (though not most) feel unprepared for domestic violence (28%). Given that these traumatic events often occur in combination, and that there are often legal obligations and protocols for addressing them, it is disturbing that so few pastors feel prepared for responding to these issues.

Catholic priests, however, are almost twice as likely as other pastors (47% vs. 21% on average) to say they felt prepared to help people who had experienced child abuse.

It is possible that these sources of trauma often involve perpetrators as well as victims who are known by the pastors, increasing their distress over the situation. It may also be that they feel called on to assess the truthfulness of what victims are telling them, or they worry that dealing with the abuse might bring further reprisals on the victim, making the situation muddier and the pastor less able to help. Further research could reveal why pastors feel less prepared to help congregants who have experienced abusive traumatic events.

MORE EXPERIENCED, MORE PREPARED

Age and tenure correlate with a sense of confidence among pastors who may be called upon to assist individuals through trauma, indicating that practice and preparedness are linked. For example, there are no cases where young Protestant pastors feel statistically significantly more prepared than older Protestant pastors.

HELPING CHURCHES FEEL PREPARED TO HANDLE TRAUMA

BY HEATHER DREW

It is never the job of a pastor, a priest or other church leaders to assess whether or not a victim is telling the truth. Church leaders are called by God to shepherd the flock that they have been given. It is their job to listen without judgement, to ask open-ended questions so that victims have safe places to share their pain and to support survivors with their practical needs. While it is not always popular or simple, it is necessary to notify local government authorities and law enforcement when allegations of child or elder abuse have surfaced. In fact, all or most church leaders—even many volunteers—are mandated reporters of child abuse. Reporting any incidents that are shared with church leaders to local authorities is essential since it is the job of law enforcement to determine the legitimacy of the allegation.

Organizations like GRACE (Godly Response to Abuse in the Christian Environment) offer helpful resources (https://www.netgrace.org/). GRACE's mission is to empower Christian communities to recognize, prevent and respond appropriately to abuse.

Another resource that churches and church leaders can use to help both victims and perpetrators is the training program *Healing the Wounds of Trauma: How the Church Can Help*. This program prepares leaders to be facilitators for small groups of people seeking healing. It focuses on Bible-based trauma healing and how churches can help victims and offenders.

(See bio on page 72.)

Though only a minority feels equipped to respond to most traumatizing events, older Protestant pastors (those 45 and older) are more likely to feel prepared for events such as domestic violence (38% vs. 26%), physical abuse (28% vs. 16%), child abuse (24% vs. 15%), witnessing death or abuse (36% vs. 25%) and suicide (38% vs. 26%). Relatedly, older Protestant pastors are more likely to have preached on trauma (56% vs. 46%) and more likely to find the Bible very helpful in their personal experiences with trauma (82% vs. 63%).

Inexperienced Protestant pastors are significantly more likely to feel unprepared to provide help for those facing racial discrimination (42% vs. 32%), homicide (61% vs. 51%) or a diagnosis with a serious medical condition (16% vs. 9%).

Older Protestant pastors are more likely than younger pastors to feel prepared for traumatic events

RESPONSIBILITY FOR THOSE WITHIN & OUTSIDE THE CHURCH

Pastors answered the question, "How much responsibility do you think churches have to help those who are dealing with a traumatic experience?" and were presented with two subjects: those inside the church (their own congregants) and those outside the church (non-members in the surrounding community). To respond regarding people in the church, they could have selected, "A lot—churches should be equipped to help congregants," "Some—they should do what they can to help congregants" or "None—this is outside the scope of what most churches can offer."

Almost without exception, pastors feel an equal or higher level of responsibility to those within the church as they feel for those in the community. Most Protestant pastors (68%) select the first option, saying that churches should be equipped to help congregants. Only a handful of Protestant pastors select the third option, saying it is outside churches' scopes to offer help to congregants dealing with trauma. Regarding those outside the church but still within its geographical

EMPATHY, NOT ADVICE
BY BRIANNA M. LEIENDECKER

Empathy is a primary requirement for those assisting people in overcoming the impact of trauma. Much of trauma care is about coming alongside. Practical advice—even great advice—is not what is needed, and offering information or direction instead of simply listening may actually slow the healing process. Knowing this can ease the pressure on caregivers.

Trauma caregivers should be chosen from church members who can be patient and compassionate with survivors because they can identify and name another person's emotions and understand their internal frame of reference. While some of us are naturally empathetic, most people can develop this critical skill.

The Bible offers several models and encouragements for empathy. It presents God as expressing a full range of emotions, including compassion, for his people (for example, Isaiah 54:8). The apostle Paul directs followers of Jesus to show empathy towards one another (Colossians 3:12), and to "rejoice with those who rejoice" and "weep with those who weep" (Romans 12:15).

BARRIERS TO EMPATHY

Empathy can be strengthened as we practice recognizing and overcoming some natural barriers and misperceptions. Most of us, for example, naturally view other people and events through our own experiences and the culture around us. We expect that what is normal for us is normal for everyone else and are often shocked when someone with a different background violates our values or ethics. Identifying assumptions like this will help us understand another's point of view.

A related barrier to empathy is hurry. It takes time and energy to understand others, so we are primed to jump to conclusions about people and situations. Think of how often people misjudge you on a poor first impression, and how your first impressions of others can linger. We also tend to group people based on our past experiences. Humans are good at recognizing patterns, and group stereotypes and labels are natural shortcuts. But such shortcuts can lead to a false sense of empathy. Becoming aware of these tendencies and taking the time for deeper conversations will enhance empathy and strengthen our relationships.

A common misperception about empathy—especially in situations of trauma, suffering and grief—is that you must have experienced a situation yourself to fully empathize with another person. But empathy does not require sharing the experience, directly or indirectly, nor is it about pretending to have had such an experience. It requires only a willingness to enter into that person's experience and walk alongside them. Empathy is not about us and what we know; it is about the other person.

TRAINING OURSELVES IN EMPATHY

When we train ourselves in empathy, we work on changing our focus from ourselves to others. Such training fosters our desire to learn about other people and consider their thoughts and feelings. We intentionally slow down and demonstrate interest in the other person, taking the time necessary to understand their experience.

Often, people suffering from significant trauma will not communicate as well with words as through non-verbal communication. We train our ears to listen not only to the other's words but also to their tone. We pay more attention to their body language and facial expressions as they express their emotions.

While personal experience of trauma is not necessary, as noted, we can enhance the development of empathy when we make full use of our memory, instincts and imagination. As we listen, we can challenge ourselves with questions: When have I felt the way this person says they are feeling? What was that like for me? How would I be feeling if I was in her shoes? What might he be hiding, fearing, or really wanting to say to me? What should I *not* say to this person right now?

Combining these questions with our awareness about our own tendency to make assumptions and jump to conclusions will help us keep our focus on the other person. Entering into their story and frame of reference, not ours, is the key to empathy.

EMPATHY & TRAUMA CARE

Being equipped and prepared to help traumatized individuals does require knowledge about trauma and grief or best practices for recovery. Honoring the vulnerability of people who are experiencing deep suffering, we draw on empathy to create safe places for them to process their experience. We try to ask open questions, listening carefully so we can avoid adding additional pain or pressure.

Demonstrating true empathy can be a costly discipline. It requires us to sacrifice time and convenience, to alter our personal schedules and reorganize our priorities. It even requires the humility to hold back our best advice so that we can come alongside those in need and invite them into healing.

(See bio on page 85.)

community, Protestant pastors are more likely to assume "some" responsibility (59%) than "a lot" (37%). Catholic priests are less likely than Protestant pastors to say a church has a high level of responsibility to help those dealing with trauma in its congregation (40% vs. 86%), even though they report a higher number of people who have come to their churches in the past six months seeking help to cope with trauma (a mean of nine and a median of six, compared to a mean of five and a median of two among Protestant pastors).

Protestant pastors are more likely to feel their church has a responsibility to help people inside their church when they are younger, non-mainline and have witnessed a traumatic event—however, these are not the same combination of characteristics that lead pastors to feel prepared to deal with trauma.

That younger Protestant pastors are more likely to take on a high level of responsibility (76% vs. 65% of older pastors feel they should take care of congregants) but still feel less prepared signals an interesting tension. Among the young, these differences may represent less relaxed standards and therefore a sense of not having met them yet. Older Protestant pastors, who typically feel more prepared, may be better able to simultaneously say they'll do what they can without feeling responsible for all contingencies.

Nearly three-quarters of non-mainline pastors (72%) and 59 percent of mainline pastors feel their churches have a high level of responsibility to care for congregants with trauma.

A personal experience of trauma makes pastors more likely to believe the Church has a duty to address trauma in the congregation and the community. Protestant pastors who have not experienced trauma are less likely to select the highest level of responsibility for those within the church (62% vs. 75% of those who've experienced trauma). When claiming responsibility to help people outside the church, the biggest difference falls between Protestant pastors who have been primary victims of traumatic events (50%) and those who have neither witnessed nor experienced a traumatic event (28%).

When a pastor says the counseling demand at his or her church is high, they are also more likely to say there is a high responsibility to equip the congregation for trauma. Protestant pastors who expect their churches be equipped for handling trauma within the congregation are more likely than those who do not hold the church responsible at the same level to have a trained counselor on staff (64% vs. 49%). The same goes for high views of the church's responsibility to help community members with trauma (69% of pastors who have a counselor on staff vs. 54% of those who don't).

Protestant pastors with a high view of the church's responsibility toward the community (37%) more often report preaching on trauma over a six-month period (an average of two times, rather than once) and receiving congregants who are seeking help with trauma (six rather than three). The same pattern goes for ministers who sense a responsibility toward their communities outside the church; this group preaches on trauma an average of two times rather than once over six months and receives more congregants who are seeking help with trauma (seven rather than four).

Protestant pastors who hold churches to a high level of responsibility toward congregants are likely to come from larger churches. Half of Protestant pastors from churches of 250 or more congregants (51%) assert that "churches should be equipped to help anyone in the community." One-third of smaller churches (32% in churches between 100 and 250 attendees and 36% in churches with fewer than 100 attendees) agrees.

Given that most Protestant pastors feel a strong responsibility to help those in their congregations going through trauma and some sense of responsibility to help those outside the church in their communities, have they prepared their churches for these responsibilities?

A personal experience of trauma makes pastors more likely to believe the church has a duty to address trauma in the congregation and the community

 **Conclusion**

WALKING THROUGH TRAUMA WITH THE SCRIPTURES

Knowing that about one-fifth of U.S. adults and churchgoers is currently suffering from a traumatic event—and that many more have experienced such an event in the past—what can Christians do? Though coping and healing is always a challenge, we see that individuals who go to their church for help with trauma are generally satisfied. There are several steps that individuals and church leaders can take to make churches places of healing.

ENTER INTO OTHERS' PAIN

Church leaders can prepare for trauma, especially for types they are less familiar with. Forms of abuse, in particular, stand out as weak areas of preparation for pastors. Pastors who feel more prepared have more congregants coming to them for help. As pastors become more familiar with shepherding people with trauma, their churches can become places where more healing happens.

POINT TO—AND KEEP POINTING TO—HOPE AND HELP

Church leaders can speak more frequently about what their church offers for trauma. Churches do not have to offer onsite staff or programs for this information to make a difference. Churches can simply say that they know some people are likely dealing with trauma and that the church can offer them referrals to counseling and programs. When pastors talk about trauma and what their churches do, more people come forward for help with trauma. That means their churches are attracting more people with trauma or encouraging people already there to get help for their suffering.

BE MINDFUL OF THE MARGINALIZED

Church leaders and congregations can be aware that people in certain vulnerable groups have a higher rate of trauma. Women, young adults, ethnic minorities and people without college degrees report a higher incidence of trauma. Churches can seek to be more representative and more understanding of these groups and increase levels of empathy and trust in their community.

SIGN UP FOR THE LONG HAUL

Church leaders and congregations can commit to patience as people heal. The recency of traumatic events makes coping harder for people who suffer from trauma. This pain fades over the course of months and years, rather than days. Being a community of healing means being a community that supports people in the long run.

REACH OUT TO THOSE WHO ARE HURTING

Once prepared to help, church leaders can reach out to the traumatized in their communities. People who have not found relief from their trauma say they are open to help from churches, even when they aren't churchgoers. That signals hope that the Church might have a role in healing them.

FIND STRENGTH IN THE BIBLE

Finally, in one of the clearest findings in this study, the Bible plays a role in healing trauma. How can you help individuals form a habit of studying the Bible, especially in times of great need? Traumatized people who have a pattern of frequent Bible use also are happier with where they are in the healing process. While this fact alone does not tell us that Bible reading causes healing, we can also look at what happens when people start or stop Bible reading because of their trauma. Given that people who start reading the Bible are more likely to experience relief than those who stop reading, we have some confidence that this recommendation is a helpful one.

We at ABS are passionate about groups healing as they encounter the Scriptures together. Such groups can help each other understand God's Word together, in a way that can make Bible reading even more helpful for coping with and healing from trauma.

We are encouraged by these findings that when church leaders take even simple steps to address trauma through their churches, congregations respond. We hope that churches continue to become communities of light and healing, not just for their congregations, but for the flourishing of the communities of which they are a part of.

Notes

1. Worldometer. "Coronoavirus Update (Live),"updated May 6, 2020, https://www.worldometers.info/coronavirus/.
2. Centers for Disease Control and Prevention, National Center for Health Statistics. "Mortality in the United States, 2017." NCHS Data Brief No. 328. November 2018. https://www.cdc.gov/nchs/products/databriefs/db328.htm.
3. U.S. Department of Housing and Urban Development, Office of Policy Development & Research. "2017 AHS [American Housing Survey] Neighborhood Description Study." 2018. https://www.huduser.gov/portal/AHS-neighborhood-description-study-2017.html#summary-tables-tab.
4. U.S. Census Bureau. "CPS Historical Time Series Table." 2018. https://www.census.gov/data/tables/time-series/demo/educational-attainment/cps-historical-time-series.html
5. A. L. Roberts, S. E. Gilman, J. Breslau, N. Breslau, and K. C. Koenen. "Race/ethnic differences in exposure to traumatic events, development of post-traumatic stress disorder, and treatment-seeking for post-traumatic stress disorder in the United States." Psychological Medicine 41, no. 1 (January 2011): 71–83. https://www.ncbi.nlm.nih.gov/pmc/articles/PMC3097040/.
6. Bita Ghafoori, Belen Barragan, Niloufar Tohidian, and Lawrence Palinkas. "Racial and Ethnic Differences in Symptom Severity of PTSD, GAD, and Depression in Trauma-Exposed, Urban, Treatment-Seeking Adults." Journal of Traumatic Stress 25, no. 1 (February 2012): 106–110. https://www.ncbi.nlm.nih.gov/pmc/articles/PMC3599779/.
7. Hobfoll, S.A. "Conservation of resources: A new attempt at conceptualizing stress." American Psychologist 44, no.3: 513–524.
8. U.S. Federal Bureau of Investigation. "FBI Releases 2017 Crime Statistics." September 24, 2018. https://www.fbi.gov/news/pressrel/press-releases/fbi-releases-2017-crime-statistics.

 **Acknowledgments**

Trauma in America was inspired by the 16,349 (and counting) trained facilitators who use *Healing the Wounds of Trauma* and the program model of the Trauma Healing Institute. These church-based caregivers have led well over 130,000 people in Bible-based healing groups in 112 nations and 148 languages through the ministry of 692 organizations. Several of these organizations, including American Bible Society, formed the Trauma Healing Alliance, and they continue to work collaboratively to bring a biblical message of hope to those who are hurting.

Robert Briggs, now interim president and CEO of American Bible Society (ABS), was among those in 2010 who heard a call from the Church and had the visionary leadership to gather a global response, leading to the launch of the Trauma Healing Institute and greatly expanding the reach of Bible-based trauma healing. Other early leaders in this effort were Dr. Bagudekia Alobeyo, Dr. Harriet Hill and John Walter. They were joined by a growing team of professionals at ABS, other national Bible Societies and our partners at SIL, Wycliffe, Seed Company and other organizations now in the Trauma Healing Alliance.

Great thanks to the current Trauma Healing team at ABS who collaborated with the research team at Barna, providing them with professional expertise that has shaped this work. Thanks to Andrew Hood, Dr. Jeff Jue, Dr. Phil Monroe and Nathan Bowman-Johnston for their leadership and guidance throughout this process. Key contributions from the Trauma Healing team are featured in sidebars by Heather Drew and Dr. Harriet Hill.

The U.S. Ministry Team gave hours to designing, analyzing, writing and editing the monograph. Dr. Jeff Fulks and Dr. John Plake led the Ministry Intelligence Team's efforts in design and analysis, while Brianna Leiendecker contributed sidebar material from her deep experience as a Trauma Healing Master Facilitator. Peter Edman served as executive editor and a key voice of experience in the world of trauma healing publications.

Outside experts including Dr. Chan Hellman and Dr. Diane Langberg also shaped our thinking about trauma, hope and healing. Thank you for your research and daily service to others.

None of our efforts at ABS would have resulted in a finished study or monograph without the consistent, exemplary partnership of the Barna team. David Kinnaman is a leader in understanding and interpreting the landscape of faith in America and around the world. His research team, led by Brooke Hempell, invested long hours in qualitative interviews, focus group meetings, survey design and data analysis. Special thanks to each member of the research team, including Daniel Copeland, Aidan Dunn, Traci Hochmuth, Pam Jacob, Savannah Kimberlin and especially to Susan Mettes, lead analyst and writer on the study.

Once the data were collected and analyzed, Barna's editorial and production teams took over. Under the capable leadership of Alyce Youngblood, the team took a bunch of numbers and told a story that reveals both the wounds of many people in America and the hope that the Church can offer, especially when churches are properly led, trained, and equipped. Thanks to Aly Hawkins and Verónica Thames for turning our idea into this monograph. Elissa Clouse managed the project while Brenda Usery managed production. With creative direction from Joe Jensen, Annette Allen designed the cover, along with the full report. Doug Brown edited the manuscript. The Trauma in America team thanks their Barna colleagues Amy Brands, Kristin Jackson, Steve McBeth, Matt Randerson, Rhesa Storms, Jess Villa and Todd White.

Finally, thanks to each of our research participants. Whether they gave an interview, participated in a focus group or responded to a detailed survey, this work is ultimately their story. We honor each of them and ask God to bring them hope and healing through skilled, caring people in the Church and through the Word.